ALSO BY CRAIG CUSTANCE

BEHIND THE BENCH: INSIDE THE MINDS OF HOCKEY'S GREATEST COACHES

THE FRANCHISE

THE BUSINESS OF
BUILDING WINNING TEAMS

CRAIG CUSTANCE

PUBLISHED BY SIMON & SCHUSTER

NEW YORK LONDON TORONTO SYDNEY NEW DELHI

A Division of Simon & Schuster, LLC
166 King Street East, Suite 300
Toronto, Ontario M5A 1J3

This Simon & Schuster Canada edition October 2024

SIMON & SCHUSTER CANADA and colophon are registered trademarks of
Simon & Schuster, LLC

Simon & Schuster: Celebrating 100 Years of Publishing in 2024

For information about special discounts for bulk purchases, please contact
Simon & Schuster Special Sales at 1-800-268-3216 or
CustomerService@simonandschuster.ca.

Interior design by Erika R. Genova

Manufactured in the United States of America

10 9 8 7 6 5 4 3 2 1

Library and Archives Canada Cataloguing in Publication

Title: The franchise : the business of building winning teams / Craig Custance
Names: Custance, Craig, author.
Description: Simon & Schuster Canada edition.
Identifiers: Canadiana (print) 20240325273 | Canadiana (ebook) 20240373693 |
    ISBN 9781668035443 (hardcover) | ISBN 9781668035450 (EPUB)
Subjects: LCSH: National Hockey League—Management. | LCSH: Hockey
    players—Selection and appointment. | LCSH: Hockey players—Trading of. |
    LCSH: Hockey players—Recruiting. | LCSH: Success.
Classification: LCC GV847 .C87 2024 | DDC 796.962/64068—dc23

ISBN 978-1-6680-3544-3
ISBN 978-1-6680-3545-0 (ebook)

For Chris Snow.
Thank you for what you taught us about living a life with
meaning, purpose, and love.

CONTENTS

THE
FRANCHISE

INTRODUCTION

I definitely wanted to see a signed document before I quit my dream job.

I was on assignment with ESPN, covering the 2017 Eastern Conference Final between the Pittsburgh Penguins and Ottawa Senators, when the contract arrived. I checked the salary. I checked the terms. Then scrolled down to the bottom for the signature from Adam Hansmann.

I signed my name next to his.

Hansmann was one of two founders of a fledgling sports media start-up called The Athletic. We'd met in Detroit at a restaurant inside the Westin Book Cadillac, where he shared his vision for the company he started with Alex Mather. My days were currently filled with morning skates, *SportsCenter* hits, late-night games, podcast recordings, breaking news, and stories filed after midnight. I loved all of it. But his idea of creating a place where writers and sports fans could slow down and dive deeper into the stories they were telling was an enticing sales pitch.

There was an even bigger appeal.

I'd get to build a staff from scratch. I'd get to manage other people passionate about writing. We would launch a group of writers in Detroit to cover the teams I grew up rooting for in a way I'd always dreamed they'd be covered.

When I ran it all by my wife, Cassie, she was sold. Plus, I was in the middle of a two-month stretch on the road covering the NHL playoffs and currently missing Little League games. This, to her, was a no-brainer. And really, it was.

When else in my career would I get an opportunity like this?

I called to formally let ESPN know I wouldn't be returning and the decision was met with curiosity. Where do you go from ESPN? There was also a request: Could you at least stick around for the Stanley Cup Final?

I couldn't. As much as it hurt missing the pinnacle of the NHL season, there was too much work to do. There were writers to hire. Stories to plan. I couldn't wait to dive in. It's an absolute rush when every decision you make feels like a young company's future is teetering on its success.

The staff in Detroit was unreal. So was the support from sports fans in the city. The early days of The Athletic were like being on a rocket ship. We launched in Detroit. We launched coverage of the NHL across the entire league. This was happening all over North America and then the United Kingdom. It was exhilarating. As the company grew, as the number of people I was working with increased, the amount I wrote decreased. Often, that's how it goes in management. The more responsibility you add, the further away you get from doing what you love. That topic would come up a lot during the reporting for this book. Eventually, you learn to appreciate the success of the people around you and hope that somehow you contributed to it in a small way.

Then, a few years later, while I was sitting in the parking lot of a small-town grocery store in Michigan, I got another call from Adam. He was offering an opportunity to manage all of our writers and editors in the NHL, college football, and baseball. It was an incredible opportunity, but it also meant I'd be managing full-time. To do it well, I'd have to stop writing.

The challenge was exciting. Leaving the job I'd done most of my career was terrifying. So was the idea of leaving regular coverage of the NHL. Not because I was a die-hard hockey person but because I loved the interaction with the people in and around the sport.

During a conversation with Tampa Bay Lightning GM Julien BriseBois, he put it better than I ever could have. He was talking about running an American Hockey League team and I teased him about how much he loved the AHL.

"Love the AHL. I love the NHL, too. They both have the same magical ingredients. The people. The people are awesome. They're high achievers, they're smart, they're passionate about the game, they're competitive people. You're always learning from whoever you're interacting with," BriseBois said. "You're always interacting with people who are excellent at what they do. That's stimulating."

He was exactly right. BriseBois worked his way up from an internship at a law firm to build a Stanley Cup champion. A guy like Lou Lamoriello went from the Providence College campus to running an NHL team and sitting on the board of the New York Yankees. Brad Treliving started his own league. Tom Dundon built a company worth billions. Meghan Duggan changed women's hockey in the United States forever. The NHL is filled with men and women like this.

The players are elite athletes who are the best in the world at what they do. The coaches are the same, too. It's also far from a perfect world and it's filled with imperfect people. That realization has become abundantly clear in recent years where the results of toxic hockey culture became public in lawsuits against the Chicago Blackhawks saying the team failed to act when informed about sexual assault allegations against former video coach Brad Aldrich during the team's 2010 Stanley Cup playoff run. Or the culture of entitlement that led to Hockey Canada leaders protecting players rather than trying to deliver justice to the victim of an alleged sexual assault involving members of the 2018 Canadian world junior hockey team. Any clear-eyed analysis of team and culture building in hockey has to acknowledge that the sport still has a long way to go, that more of these stories may be woven throughout the history of the game.

But in reporting this book I saw so much opportunity. I saw a chance to learn from some of the smartest people in the game in a way that was very relevant to the job I was taking on. And at its heart, it's an attempt to bring those insights, strategies, stories, and wisdom to anyone interested in learning a little more about how the best do what they do.

My sincere hope is that you're able to discover a few of those magical ingredients in these pages.

CHAPTER 1

THE POWER OF RELENTLESS PREPARATION

That's it. That's all I care about. Those are the only things that really bring me happiness.

—**Julien BriseBois**

I was sore. Not hit-by-a-truck sore, but my legs were starting to tighten and there was a slight pain in my lower back. What concerned me, while writing next to a pool at the Channelside Marriott in Tampa, was that I knew enough about athletic exertion to understand that what I did that morning should have absolutely zero physical impact a few hours later on my body.

Pickleball, by its nature, isn't a strenuous sport. If you haven't played, it's essentially a mix of tennis and ping-pong. Until the last several years, best I can tell, it's been played mostly by seniors. But one thing that happened during the NHL playoff bubble of 2020 is that teams and their staff played *a lot* of it. In that same time frame, my wife and I found it a great way to get outside and spend time with some of our close friends during an era in which you couldn't interact otherwise. I actually started thinking I was getting pretty good at it.

Julien BriseBois ended that illusion.

Julien, who won back-to-back Stanley Cups as general manager of the Tampa Bay Lightning in 2020 and 2021, has one of the most fascinating paths to success of any NHL GM. He arrived at Heenan Blaikie, a Quebec law firm, as an intern hoping to one day become a tax lawyer. He grew up playing baseball. In a sport filled with former hockey players running teams, he's not that. But he was trained by two of the best. In that 2020 NHL playoff bubble, created because it was being played during a global pandemic, he ended up raising the Stanley Cup. Then his team won it again the following season. All while honing his pickleball game.

He's thoughtful. He's analytical. He's the kind of person I love chatting with.

My initial pitch was to spend the day together with the Stanley Cup in Montreal. But there were travel bans and limits on people who could join him. All the things we dealt with in 2020. So months later, I circled back. His Lightning were facing the Florida Panthers in the first round of the 2021 Stanley Cup playoffs, the first time these two Florida rivals competed in the playoffs. It seemed like a good time to go to Florida.

"Come down and let's play pickleball," he suggested.

I didn't consider the idea nearly long enough. At that moment, I didn't know Julien had been playing it for years. That he also boxes for fun. That he doesn't drink or smoke. That he is a believer that a healthy body means a healthy mind. That he has the wingspan of an oversized condor. Why would I know any of this?

"Let's do it."

═══════════════════

It was the morning of the day before our pickleball showdown and I regretted a couple of things. One, that I never shed my quarantine weight. And two, that I waited so long to prepare. My solution was to go for a light jog outside the Marriott along the channel in Tampa. It was 9:30 a.m. and already hot. At least hot for someone who was coming from a prolonged Michigan winter. The smallest of hills slowed me down. I was not feeling great about any of this.

A few minutes after I returned to my hotel room, my phone rang.

It was the Honorable Daniel Dumais, a judge in the Superior Court in Quebec. But before that he was a lawyer at Heenan Blaikie, then considered one of the best sports law firms in Canada. He had NHL teams as clients, and in some ways, he was the guy who launched BriseBois into the hockey universe.

I answered and explained what I was doing. That I wanted to get to know BriseBois's backstory a little better before we had an extended conversation. That Julien had mentioned him as one of his biggest mentors.

"Anything for my friend Julien."

Dumais started describing Julien and he was doing it through the lens of someone who has known him for years, who knows him as well as anyone. Who knew him at the start. But as he kept talking, I thought only of what it meant to me, his pickleball opponent.

"Julien is very serious," Dumais explained. "He's very committed to whatever he does. He's structured, he has a plan. Julien is someone who has an idea, what he wants to do, what he wants to achieve."

Dumais was in charge of the firm's NHL work—arbitration cases and salary negotiations—and after BriseBois joined the firm as an intern, he let him know that there were boxes in the archives with all the firm's work in sports, the decisions on arbitrations that had been awarded over the past decade. So that evening, Brise-Bois found the boxes and got to work.

He started indexing each case. He built out a binder for easy access to the decisions in an organized way. During the day, he was working on his regular assignments. In the morning and at night, he was organizing years of arbitration cases. Dumais and BriseBois didn't cross paths for a month. But when they finally did, BriseBois pulled out the binder that took a decade to accumulate and showed it to Dumais.

"I'm ready to call GMs whenever you're ready," BriseBois said.

He was twenty-two.

"He didn't say anything. He just took it and left. But I knew I impressed him," BriseBois said. "I had to. It was impressive work, I have to say."

So they started cold-calling general managers and the business started to grow. Nobody knew it was a twenty-two-year-old intern on the other end of the line, just somebody who NHL teams started to believe could help them win arbitration cases. A few weeks later, a group of NHL executives flew to Quebec City so they could work together in person. They gathered in a conference room and started going over all the arbitration cases.

For the first few hours BriseBois was quiet, but right before lunch, Anaheim Ducks GM Pierre Gauthier looked over at him and asked him what he thought.

As BriseBois does, he shared his well-prepared opinions with confidence.

"'This is what we should do for this because of this award and that award. This is the number for your guy, that guy. This is the number for your guy,'" BriseBois said in recalling that moment. "And then Pierre said, 'That sounds awesome. Let's grab lunch.'"

Word traveled fast about the arbitration cases this firm was helping teams win. Since Disney owned both the Ducks and the Angels, the success spread into the baseball world. That winter, the firm started doing arbitration cases for the Royals and the first general managers meeting BriseBois ever attended was in baseball. He was now working in the Montreal office, so Dumais told him to meet him in Washington, D.C., at Dulles Airport, where the MLB managers were gathering. A snowstorm wiped out Dumais's flight, so BriseBois, now twenty-three, was the lone representative from the firm. He walked into a conference room where baseball general managers, most decades older than he was, were going over a list of players eligible for arbitration. At one point, an opposing general manager suggested paying his player an extra half million more than planned. It was put to a vote.

Who thinks it should be the higher number?

The lone GM raised his hand.

Who thinks it should be the old number?

Every other hand went up.

Royals GM Allard Baird leaned over to BriseBois and shifted strategies.

"Julien, when it's our turn, you do the talking."

BriseBois laughed hard retelling that story.

The one thing you learn about BriseBois is that he's very intentional in his actions, especially when it comes to his career path. Even when he wanted to become a general manager, he didn't interview for every opening, despite outside interest. He was willing to be patient for the right situation. He was willing to take risks to improve the likelihood that the right situation would present itself.

When it was clear tax law wasn't going to be his future, he changed gears quickly. When he saw an opportunity with the Montreal Canadiens to work on contracts while he was still with the law firm, he took full advantage, and it didn't take long for everyone to realize he wasn't going back to the firm. Martin Madden, a former general manager of the Quebec Nordiques, had the office next door at the Bell Centre and immediately noticed how at ease BriseBois was around the rest of the staff. His relentless preparation mixed with his curiosity gave him a confidence to learn quickly in this environment.

"It felt easy for me to sit down with him and discuss hockey, how I felt the game should be played, how it should be managed, and it started that way," Madden said. "There wasn't a day in the year that we didn't discuss his point of view and how I thought things should go. He was always asking questions and, most of the time, had some real good answers."

After BriseBois joined the Canadiens full-time, GM André Savard said he was intentional about giving BriseBois opportunities on the road with the team, the best way to learn the sport.

He also realized quickly that BriseBois was somebody you had to challenge. He was ambitious and learned quickly, and Savard looked for ways to feed that drive.

It came by getting him out of the office.

"It didn't take me too long, a month. I realized, 'Get him involved more,'" Savard said. "I had enough confidence in him to put him in that situation. When you go on the road, on the plane, you're going after the games, you go see the coaches in the morning practice, you talk to the coaches, there's a lot of conversations there. There's a lot of communication between everybody going on the road. I thought that was important."

BriseBois's immersion into the world of hockey with the Montreal Canadiens expanded under GM Bob Gainey, who put him in charge of the Canadiens' American Hockey League franchise in 2006. Gainey walked into BriseBois's office, told him Hamilton needed a GM and he believed it should be BriseBois. Then he acted like he was handing him the keys.

"He said, 'Go compete with the other guys. Show me what you can do,'" BriseBois said. "And he left."

The Hamilton Bulldogs would win a Calder Cup in 2007. Eight years into his time with the Canadiens, BriseBois started to realize that further growth would mean leaving this comfort zone. He wanted to expand his hockey network. He wanted to learn from new mentors. He wanted to build on the success he had in running the Canadiens AHL team in Hamilton. It was the summer of 2009 and the Canadiens had a long list of free agents that needed new deals. BriseBois's contract was also expiring, so he went to Gainey to propose an exit strategy. He'd extend his own deal by one year, help work on contract negotiations for guys like Saku Koivu, Alexei Kovalev, and Mike Komisarek. Then, as the year progressed, he said he'd help the Canadiens hire a replacement, work on the transition, and then figure out what was next.

"Let's keep that between us for now," Gainey answered. "You may want to change your mind."

Gainey suggested they do the one-year deal, reconvene during the season, and go from there. But when BriseBois went to him during the season to figure out the best path forward, Gainey put him off. BriseBois tried to connect multiple times, and was unsuccessful each time. Gainey was buying time, but finally relented. He invited BriseBois to breakfast at his home and BriseBois laid it all out.

It's time for me to go. It's time for me to learn from other people and from organizations that aren't as unique as the Montreal Canadiens.

"Well," Gainey answered, "it's time for me to go, too. I resigned in December."

He let BriseBois know that the plan was to promote Pierre Gauthier to the GM spot.

This complicated BriseBois's plans because Gauthier was crucial to his development as an executive. When he first started working in the NHL, BriseBois reached out to a group of people he trusted and asked for advice on how to be the best assistant GM. David Poile gave him great advice. So did Ray Shero. But Gauthier wrote a three-page memo, in a small font, loaded with career advice. BriseBois still has it. So now BriseBois was concerned that it would look like he didn't want to work for Gauthier if he left. Gainey let Gauthier know about BriseBois's concerns and Gauthier went out of his way to help with the transition.

"I understand. I was you once and I did the same thing," Gauthier told BriseBois. "I felt like I needed to leave the Nordiques. I fully understand what you're doing and it's probably the right thing for your career."

The timing was right, too. The AHL team BriseBois built in Hamilton was going well. The coach he hired, Guy Boucher, was looking like a really smart choice. He had the development program in place that took years to build. Because of it, BriseBois's reputation in the NHL had grown enough that when the Tampa Bay Lightning had a GM opening that offseason under new owner Jeff Vinik, BriseBois got a screening call from Jac Sperling, who was doing the vetting for the open job.

"I think they had a very long list of candidates, they may have had thirty names," BriseBois said. "I might have been thirtieth on the list."

Eventually, the Lightning hired Steve Yzerman away from the Detroit Red Wings' front office, which meant Yzerman needed an assistant. It was the perfect job for BriseBois, but word was circulating that it might go to Ryan Martin, who Yzerman worked with in Detroit. When BriseBois and Martin chatted on the phone, Martin confirmed the speculation.

"Steve has offered me the job, I'm going to go to Tampa with him," Martin said.

BriseBois congratulated him. He let him know how highly he felt about that opportunity under Yzerman, and Martin picked up a hint of disappointment. BriseBois filled him in. He told him he was leaving Montreal and was looking for a job. He let him know that was one he thought was probably the best.

"Ryan being the incredible guy he is says, 'Well, I've got that job, but if something happens, I will tell Stevie he should hire you,'" BriseBois said.

About a month went by and BriseBois was doing dishes at his house in Montreal. It was about 9 p.m. when his phone rang.

Ryan Martin was on the other end of the line.

Martin had agonized over the decision. He'd had several conversations with mentors Ken Holland and Jim Nill in Detroit about staying with the Red Wings. His wife's job would have to change, too, if he moved to Florida. His role in Detroit was expanding, so was his paycheck, and the opportunity to scout nearby games at all levels and be home with his family was an important factor. It all added up.

"I changed my mind," Martin said when we chatted years later. "I know there had been a couple other people who had reached out to Steve, but I gave my opinion of Julien that they would work well together."

Shortly after that, Yzerman reached out to Gauthier for permission to interview BriseBois, and the conversations started. During the day, BriseBois worked for the Canadiens. At night, he talked to Yzerman. For well over a week, they followed the same routine. Every night around nine or ten o'clock, Yzerman would let BriseBois know what he was working on and BriseBois would offer his thoughts.

Eventually the two decided they should meet. BriseBois was going to Hilton Head for the AHL board of governors meeting, but was able to find a flight to Tampa that gave him a five-hour window to meet Yzerman in person at the airport Westin. BriseBois brought a presentation he'd created around team building and the core competencies he believed every organization needed, especially around player procurement and development. The deck broke down what he was able to do along those lines in Hamilton, where he believed the team needed more coaches. In his mind, the AHL is where a player is getting his PhD in hockey and he thought there needed to be a better student-to-teacher ratio than hockey typically allowed. In Hamilton, they added a full-time strength coach. They added a full-time video coach. He worked on bringing in the right veterans to surround the young guys, show them how to be a professional, how to conduct yourself.

"All the pieces kind of fell into place," BriseBois said.

The pitch worked. On July 16, 2010, BriseBois was named the assistant GM. And almost immediately, BriseBois's preparation and willingness to take a risk would pay off in a big way.

───────────────────────────

The interview was nearly over.

BriseBois had taken the candidate to coach Tampa Bay's AHL team through a binder full of questions he had prepared, while Yzerman injected his own questions as the conversation needed it. Now, apparently satisfied, they had just one more question.

They turned a screen toward the young candidate, who had never coached a single game higher than junior hockey in the United States, a guy who had spent more time as a lawyer than a professional coach, and hit play. A commercial kicked on and the candidate immediately knew what it was. It was a knockoff of the old Dos Equis commercials featuring the Most Interesting Man in the World.

Only this time, the title says "The Most Interesting Man in Hockey."

A Spanish guitar plays while a camera pans past a table full of beautiful women until it focuses in on the man at the end of the table next to a martini.

It's Green Bay coach Jon Cooper.

Cooper looks at the camera, says, "Find out what it is in hockey you don't do well. . . ." He pauses and leans forward slightly. "And don't do that thing."

It was an advertisement for the Green Bay Gamblers, a team that had just won a championship with Cooper behind the bench. It was a job that Cooper figured he'd keep the rest of his career. He had just won a championship. He got a raise that paid him six figures. He even had a golf membership. He was pretty content with where his career had landed. But when Newport agent Wade Arnott suggested to Yzerman and BriseBois that they should consider the coach in Green Bay they'd never heard of, that future changed.

Even as BriseBois took him through his binder full of questions during the interview, Cooper didn't think this job was happening. It wasn't until the commercial was played and one of them ended it with: Do you *really* think you're the most interesting man in hockey—that's when he started to suspect he might have a shot.

They were having fun with him and that's usually a good sign in an interview.

"If they didn't like me, they wouldn't have shown it," Cooper explained while sharing the story. "They were looking to see if I could take it."

Cooper had a flight to catch that was getting dangerously close, so BriseBois offered to drive him to the airport. They hustled to his car, where BriseBois tried making a phone call without success. Cooper sensed frustration.

"He goes, 'To be honest, I don't know how to fucking get to the airport,'" Cooper said, laughing. "I start laughing so hard, and say, 'Let's navigate.' He drops me off, the airplane door hits my ass on the way in, that's how close I came to missing it."

But Cooper noticed that BriseBois was using every available minute to assess the guy he was considering as his AHL coach. He volunteered to drive him to the airport, even if he didn't know the route. It's a strategy Cooper has now adopted when there's a new player or staff member who needs a lift. That car time is invaluable. In fact, when I called Cooper to talk about BriseBois, he was on the way home from the airport after dropping off the team's mental performance coach.

"I took that from Julien," Cooper said. "It's a side of caring, getting to know someone and relationship building."

When he got on the plane, Cooper called his wife. He still felt like the AHL job was a long shot, since the jump from Green Bay to a head spot in the AHL was big, but he thought things were closer than they were the day before.

"I gave them something to think about," he told his wife.

Less than forty-eight hours later, BriseBois was on the phone offering him the job. When Tampa got the money where it needed to be, Cooper decided to go for it. Even if it meant losing the golf club membership and arguably the best local ad campaign hockey has seen.

"That was when I threw caution to the wind," Cooper said. "In the end, this is your chance. I didn't want to leave Green Bay, but I saw this as an opportunity."

That the interview with BriseBois started with a list of twenty-five or so questions he was reading directly out of a binder was very much by design. So was the intentional decision to wait until the end of the interview to break the ice.

BriseBois's hiring record on coaches is remarkably strong.

He hired an unknown named Guy Boucher in Hamilton, who went on to take the Tampa Bay Lightning to the Eastern Conference Final in 2011. He hired Cooper in Norfolk, and Cooper will end up in the Hall of Fame. He hired Benoit Groulx to replace Cooper, and he ended with the most wins by a Syracuse coach in franchise history, taking the team to the playoffs every season he was there.

BriseBois has a very defined process he uses to make hires and it's clear by his history that it's a good one. It's a topic I was eager to explore after getting run all over a Florida pickleball court.

―――――――――――

It had been three games and I could barely breathe. I was sweating through my Torchy's Tacos T-shirt, and when I looked over at Julien, he'd barely broken a sweat.

I started looking for an exit strategy.

"Is there somewhere we can go to chat?" I asked, taking a seat on the bench next to the pickleball court.

"Do you want one more?"

Julien wanted to keep playing.

"Your call," he said. "Can your body take one more?"

He was now going after my pride. I told him I'd keep going if he wanted to keep playing but it was clear my heart wasn't in it.

"All right, we're done," he answered. "What do you like to drink? I'm a cold soda type of guy."

We packed our gear and walked toward his car. As always, he was prepared with a change of clothes, an idea that never even occurred to me until that moment. He said a place called Buddy

Brew had great iced tea. In his first sign of mercy of the morning, he turned up the air-conditioning in his car before pulling away from the park.

His cold soda comment sparked a thought. When you cover enough general managers meetings or board of governors meetings, you end up crossing paths with NHL management in hotel bars or enjoying a glass of wine at a nearby restaurant. But Julien was always a guy you'd more likely see ducking out of these events with a tennis bag than posting up at the bar.

I'd heard he didn't drink alcohol and was wondering what went behind the decision.

"I never started," he said.

Then he shared a story that explained it a little more. In his earliest days, when he was showing up to work at a law firm starting at 7 a.m. and working until midnight, his dad was playing hockey more often with his close friends than he was able to play. The work-life balance didn't seem right. He realized that there were three things in his life that brought him happiness. Time with his immediate family. Investing in his career. And doing something physical on the weekends.

"That's it. That's all I care about. Those are the only things that really bring me happiness," he said. "To this day, it's the same thing. I remember telling Steve [Yzerman] that and he goes, 'I'm exactly the same way.' And he is. So that's what I do."

It's that simple. Each of these three areas of his life are working toward a goal. A strong family. A successful career. Physical exhaustion. Anything else seems to just get in the way.

"Everyone can do the easy stuff. There's no satisfaction that comes with the easy stuff," he said. "Our pickleball match may not have been the best example, but had you pushed me to my limits there would be a sense of satisfaction that comes from being exhausted. I accomplished something that not everyone—"

"Not everyone beats me, Julien."

"I know. So yeah, if you're going to go into the gym, make it count. If it's short, it's intense. If it's long, it's heavy. When you're done, you want to feel like you've accomplished something."

He parked the car and we walked around to the front of the coffee shop, entering Buddy Brew as "Call Me Maybe" played in the background. I ordered an iced tea. He got an iced mocha latte and we found a seat outside.

This was when we really dug in.

Even the most intelligent, driven people aren't going to find success without opportunity, without someone willing to invest in them. BriseBois always seems keenly aware of that. When he talks about his time in the law firm, it isn't just about the extra work he put in. It's the guidance and opportunity Dumais provided. When he talks about his success in Tampa Bay, he's quick to credit owner Jeff Vinik and Steve Yzerman for building an environment conducive to success. He also seems like someone who, if he didn't have those things, is willing to change jobs until he does. Who he's working for is every bit as important as where he's working.

So when our conversation shifted into his hiring process, he began by crediting Bob Gainey. Gainey was the GM in Montreal when the Hamilton Bulldogs needed a new head coach in 2009, and it would have been easy for him to micromanage the process. BriseBois went to Gainey for insight, and while Gainey was there for guidance, this was going to be BriseBois's call completely.

"Now, you have to be a really strong, confident, and secure person to be the GM of the Montreal Canadiens and be willing to let one of your underlings in that market make mistakes there," BriseBois said. "Sometimes he knew I was making a mistake and he still let me make the mistake. You need someone special to do that. He wanted this to be my process."

So BriseBois went to work. He was looking for someone progressive, who saw the game the same way he did. He wanted someone whose focus was on education and teaching as much as it was winning games. He wanted someone focused on player development for the Montreal Canadiens rather than someone just trying to grind out an AHL win.

One of the people who BriseBois got to know while getting his MBA was a guy named André Couillard, now the president of Procom Quebec. Couillard has a great eye for talent and has helped guide people through the hiring process in the world of information and communications technology. BriseBois called Couillard and told him he was about to make his first big hire, a head coach for the Hamilton Bulldogs. He started by asking: What are the mistakes people make when they hire?

"He gave me an education," BriseBois said.

In an ideal world, you hire someone for three or six months and watch them do the job. See how they operate. See how they solve problems. If you're able to do this a few times, you find the ideal candidate. Hockey doesn't work that way. The next best thing is to try to simulate that scenario.

That means digging into how a candidate did in their previous job. If it's a coach, you talk to their players. You talk to their managers. You talk to their opponents. You try to learn as much as possible about how they operate. Then you use the interview process to put them in the chair of the job you're filling. In this case, the coach of the Hamilton Bulldogs. You're not using the interview process to get to know the candidate personally. You want to find out how they'll act once they get the job.

"So you throw situations at them," BriseBois said. "And you don't want to get to know the person until you know the coach. People start getting friendly, start getting to know each other—'Oh, you play tennis? I play tennis, too.' The interview is over. You've already broken it. It's broken beyond repair. Avoid that."

Instead, it's always the same process, one he shaped with insight from Couillard. Here is the job. Here is the mandate. This is the pay range. Still interested? Okay, then here are some scenarios. BriseBois takes his candidates through open-ended questions in which there are no right or wrong answers. Each coach gets the same group of questions. That binder BriseBois was running through with Yzerman when he interviewed Cooper? It featured these scenarios.

BriseBois shared an example.

Training camp is about to end. You're going to keep fourteen forwards. Thirteen are no-brainers. We're down to two guys for one open job. One guy is not the most skilled guy, but he's super gritty, competes. He works his butt off in practice every day. Will always try his hardest to give you what you want, but he's very limited as a skill player. The other guy? High-end skill. Effort isn't always there. You have to get it out of him. Which guy are you keeping and why?

Do this twenty times and you get to know your candidate well. Then the personal questions can begin. Like, do you really think you're the most interesting man in the world?

"I will say, by the end, they're exhausted," BriseBois said. "Whoever I'm interviewing, they need a nap. That's what I did with Guy that year. The process has to be identical for every guy. Same room. Same time of day. Same questions in the same order. You don't compare notes with anyone until the end. You put it in writing. There's a process to try and avoid the mistakes that are made because of our unconscious biases."

For his interview with BriseBois in 2016, Benoit Groulx remembered meeting him around 1 p.m. at a hotel in New York. It was a beautiful spring afternoon in Manhattan and Groulx noticed that BriseBois was wearing running shoes.

"You like walking? Let's go for a walk," BriseBois said.

They walked toward Bryant Park before finding a table a few blocks away. They sat down, BriseBois pulled out a tablet, and here came the scenarios.

"He bombarded me with all kinds of questions," Groulx told me. "Many, many different situations."

By the time Groulx got back to his hotel around 11 p.m., he was exhausted. The next morning, Steve Yzerman picked him up for a walk and then a lunch. It was a different conversation, but Groulx left it thinking that the two managers really complemented each other well.

"Two smart guys, but they're different," Groulx said. "I knew why that team was successful."

It wasn't the interview process that left the most lasting impression on Groulx during his time working for BriseBois. It was how clearly BriseBois set expectations once he hired the coaching staff. Groulx still has the paper that broke down BriseBois's expectations about the team in Syracuse. They were guiding principles for the organization, principles behind every decision that Groulx and his staff made. It starts with a clear mandate. Then it breaks down how the organization sets the culture and the kind of behavior that is expected from everyone on the team. It includes twelve steps on how to develop the team.

BriseBois sat down with the coaches and explained the mission and then backed it up in written form. Groulx kept it in his office and referred to it often, sometimes more than once in the same day. I sent BriseBois an email asking for a copy. Two days later, my phone was buzzing with his name on the screen. Yes, he still had a copy. No, it wasn't going to be published somewhere everybody could read it.

"It's still too much in use," he said.

Like so many things BriseBois does, this organizational source of truth was him being proactive. He wanted something in writing to guide decisions when stress is high and when decisions aren't always made with a clear head.

"When it's written, you have something you can refer to," he explained. "When it's written, you've taken the time to select the words we're using. This deck guides all the decisions. Your job is to be disciplined enough to refer to the deck and not waver. This is what we do, this is what we believe in. When we were not feeling the heat, when we were calm and rational, this was the road map to sustained success."

For seven seasons, that's exactly what Groulx had in Syracuse. Two hundred fifty-six wins. Two division titles. An Eastern Conference championship. More wins than any coach in franchise history.

But BriseBois decided the team needed a fresh voice in the AHL and he was out. Groulx was considering leaving the organization after one more season but didn't get that chance. If you learn anything about BriseBois, you need to know this: he'd rather move on too early than too late.

He can be ruthless in how decisive he is. Once all the proper steps are completed and a decision is made, he moves. No matter how it might look from the outside, something the hockey world would learn as his tenure in Tampa Bay continued.

———————————

The 2023 NHL trade deadline was closing in and BriseBois agreed to catch up over a coffee at the Lightning's road hotel in Detroit. The Lightning had won another Stanley Cup since he steamrolled me on the pickleball court a couple years earlier, this time beating the Montreal Canadiens in the Stanley Cup Final, a serendipitous twist to the BriseBois legacy. The following season, BriseBois's Lightning advanced to a third Stanley Cup Final in three years, one of the most remarkable accomplishments in the salary cap era. They lost to a Colorado Avalanche team built to dethrone them.

I was waiting near some couches in the hotel lobby a few feet away from Lightning assistant GM Mathieu Darche, who was on the phone. I didn't know it in the moment, but BriseBois, Darche, and the Lightning front office were working on a trade deadline deal that might have been their most bold yet.

Shortly after I arrived, BriseBois turned the corner.

"How's your pickleball game?" he asked.

It was not great.

His, however, was improving. He'd hired a pickleball pro to train him, doing it because he believes that striving to get better at these skills is a healthy way to live. He was investing more into equipment, explaining that paddle design and evolution had improved considerably in the last year. As with everything, he was constantly looking for small, incremental improvements.

"These new carbon paddles, they fit my stroke," he said. "I put a lot of top spin on it and they add top spin. There's going to be a little bit more power. There's something there. I'm excited."

I was catching BriseBois at an interesting time. He had a team built to win a Stanley Cup and he'd now gotten in the habit of making a move near the trade deadline to help push his team there. Three straight years he'd made big moves and three straight years he'd advanced to the Stanley Cup Final. The strategy was paying off and it was also an adjustment in how he operated.

In 2019, the Tampa Bay Lightning didn't do anything at the trade deadline, which is the most rational approach. The way BriseBois calculates the odds, he figures his team has a 6 or 7 percent shot at winning the Stanley Cup. If you're someone who is always thinking of the future, the idea of using valuable draft capital to trade for players who might only be on the team for a few months during a playoff run that is a coin toss away from ending isn't a great one. BriseBois believed that, mathematically, doing nothing changes the Stanley Cup odds about as much as a major trade. And in 2019, the Lightning kept winning in the regular season, tying the 1995–96 Detroit Red Wings for the most wins in the history of the game during the regular season. They played four postseason games that year and lost them all, swept by the Columbus Blue Jackets.

That offseason, he had to make a decision about how to respond to the collapse in the playoffs. It certainly would have been understandable to make a change at coach. Or maybe trade one of the underperforming skill players. Really, he could have done anything following the loss to the Blue Jackets and been publicly justified. Instead, he brought everybody back. Part of him believed that if that series was played one hundred times, the Lightning would have had a much different outcome in many of those series. It just turned out that reality included a sweep.

"It really, really sucked and hurt and we ended up drawing the one where we got spanked, and we didn't even look good doing it. They played great and we didn't put our best foot forward," BriseBois said. "That's all it was. It was seven days."

He believed in his team and coach. In this case, accountability meant sending the same group out there to do it again.

"We *had* to come back. If we had made changes, we would have let too many people off the hook. This was a collective fail, we all had to come back," he explained. "If you change one or two players—it's those guys. No, no, it's all of us. And it *was* all of us. It was a collective failure."

While the roster stayed essentially the same heading into the next season, there were changes. One was how Jon Cooper held his top players accountable with ice time. The second was how BriseBois approached the following trade deadline and the deadlines to come.

"What it did for Julien, it changed his mentality of what you trade for at the deadline," Cooper said.

There are three assets a general manager has when building a team. Draft picks, cap space, and players on the reserve list. Of the three, the one thing the Lightning valued most while looking to improve their roster in 2020 was cap space. They had great players. They were trying to win now, so draft picks weren't as valuable.

"What we were looking to do was buy cap space. We tried to

do that, but couldn't. The other avenue is undervalued players—players worth more than their cap number is the same result."

Acquiring undervalued players is another form of adding cap space.

"Essentially, yeah," BriseBois said. "If you're going to buy at the deadline and pay those prices, odds are, it's not going to work. Presidents' Trophy winners are more likely to lose in the first round than win the Cup. We know from experience."

So they set out to find players that checked these boxes: Undervalued contracts with term remaining. Players who fit needs in the lineup.

In 2020, those players were Barclay Goodrow and Blake Coleman, players who BriseBois felt were worth much more to the Lightning than their cap hit suggested. They fit needs and would be around more than just the one postseason. In both cases BriseBois paid a premium.

"We got it to a place where I was more comfortable living with the regret of doing the trade and not having it work out than not doing the trade, not winning, and then forever asking myself, 'What if I'd done the trade, would I be a Stanley Cup winner?' That's what it comes down to," he said.

In 2021, they acquired a more traditional trade deadline rental in defenseman David Savard, but BriseBois felt he had good reason. Star forward Nikita Kucherov had missed the entire regular season following hip surgery, so the Lightning were able to use his cap space elsewhere. They were also getting positive reports that he might be able to return for the playoffs, where the salary cap doesn't apply. This was already a loaded team, with only one real need, in BriseBois's assessment—a right-shot defenseman. Getting Savard at a salary discount by laundering him through Detroit set up the Lightning for a massive postseason advantage. Since Kucherov's $9.5 million cap hit wouldn't count, adding Savard at 25 percent of his salary to a team that could already go well over the regular season cap when Kucherov returned put the Lightning in a unique position.

"The way [long-term injured reserve] worked, I am already working off a ninety-million-dollar cap. I'll have a ninety-million-dollar team competing against eighty-million-dollar teams," BriseBois said. "We already have an advantage, let's push even more chips. Let's make sure we take advantage of this opportunity. Let's get someone else to pay, because I got Savard for a million bucks. It's a four-million-dollar player I'm getting for a million bucks."

The Lightning would go on to win another Stanley Cup with one of the best rosters assembled in the cap era, using every possible dollar and rule to their advantage. Opponents noticed.

"We lost to a team that's eighteen million dollars over the cap, or whatever they are," Hurricanes defenseman Dougie Hamilton said after his season was ended by the Lightning. It was enough of an advantage that the NHL investigated to make sure there wasn't anything done on the Kucherov front against the rules. They found no wrongdoing.

"At the deadline, I went, 'We have an unreal team. If Kuch is back and he is Kuch and he's looking like he will, we have no holes,'" BriseBois said.

It worked.

BriseBois is creative, decisive, and willing to use every rule to his advantage when building his team. He's also just as decisive when he has to make difficult changes. This was especially evident with the trade of Ryan McDonagh to the Nashville Predators in the 2022 offseason. This move falls under the category of BriseBois preferring to make a move too early than pay the price for waiting too long. He was being proactive because McDonagh's $6.75 million in cap space would eventually be needed to sign Mikhail Sergachev, Anthony Cirelli, and Erik Cernak. McDonagh had a no-trade clause in his deal that still had four more seasons, but BriseBois also had leverage. If McDonagh didn't accept the trade to Nashville, he would be put on waivers, where there were teams in line to claim him.

This is the kind of move where BriseBois has to walk the uncomfortable line between ruthless and empathetic. He doesn't deny that he was willing to put McDonagh on waivers. He believes it was the right thing for the organization. He also knows that his name isn't on the Stanley Cup without Ryan McDonagh, someone who bled for the organization.

"You're dealing with a high-character, highly professional, mature person who's been around. I'm sure it was shitty. I know his wife. She's awesome. Kaylee," BriseBois said.

Then there was a long pause.

"They and our guys all have, they all for the most part—especially our veteran, more established guys—all live on the same street. Like, they literally golf cart to each other's house. The kids all play on the same T-ball teams or Learn to Skate teams. It's a tight group. So I knew the repercussions of all that."

And still made the deal.

There are times when leading an organization can be lonely. This trade probably didn't get a lot of support from the coaches. It was a leader having the most difficult of conversations because he truly believed it put the organization in the best position moving forward. The moment you can't make those tough moves, Vegas president George McPhee would say later, is the moment you should no longer be running a team.

It doesn't make it any easier.

"It's not about me in that moment," BriseBois said. "I never lose sight of that. I don't pity myself in that situation. I feel for the other person more than I do for myself. I'm doing my job. They're the victims of me doing my job."

There's a book by management consultant Olivier Sibony called *You're About to Make a Terrible Mistake*. It's a book about how biases can distort the decision-making process for even the top people in business. The book features case studies on those mistakes and solutions on how to create organizational processes to help collect information that might avoid as many mistakes as possible.

Prior to the 2023 trade deadline, BriseBois sent a message to the group text chain for his front office recommending that they read this book. It might be the perfect book title for any NHL team's trade deadline, a time filled with short-term bias and where processes pay off. A few days after we chatted before the 2023 deadline, BriseBois traded defenseman Cal Foote, a 2025 first-round pick, and four other draft picks to the Nashville Predators for forward Tanner Jeannot. It was a steep price to pay for a guy who only had five goals for the Predators when he was dealt. This was BriseBois tripling down on the trade deadline theory of acquiring a player he believed was worth more than his cap charge and do it with someone who will be around a couple years.

But now, three years after using that strategy successfully to acquire Goodrow and Coleman, BriseBois had competition in trying to strike a deal like this. Jeannot wasn't a player the Predators were eager to trade. He had the leadership and work-ethic qualities that then-GM David Poile felt like the organization needed to help bridge the gap through roster reconstruction. He also had a style of play conducive to postseason success. All the reasons Poile wanted to keep him made him a major target for contenders.

"The most calls I had was on Tanner Jeannot," Poile said. "Everybody wanted him."

So Poile set a high price. He told every GM who called that it would cost two first-round picks to acquire him from the Predators. Multiple teams offered a first-round pick and prospects, but nobody reached the asking price. And then BriseBois called.

"He has no cap space, he has no younger players who were of interest to me. He had no first-round pick this season. I just looked and said, 'Here's your draft picks. You have a first in '25, a second in '24, a third, fourth, and fifth. I think that's equivalent to two first-round picks."

They made the deal.

"We'll attach names to those picks someday and we'll actually know how it turned out," Poile said.

Poile has talked to BriseBois as much as any GM in the league through the years. Sometimes about trades, but more often BriseBois was just trying to tap into Poile's years of experience. Why did you make this move? How did you handle that issue?

"Julien separates himself from the other ones. He is calling everybody. He is asking about situations. I'm just answering questions," Poile said.

And he's answering from his experience and from those who preceded him. Poile was mentored by Cliff Fletcher, Glen Sather, Emile Francis, and Harry Sinden, among others, through the years, and whether he knew it or not, BriseBois was getting their experiences as well in Poile's answers. Poile was there at the start of BriseBois's career. He spent time with the intern version of BriseBois while he was doing Predators arbitration cases for Dumais. He saw a kid who was very smart and very prepared.

"Little did I know or think this was his passion," Poile said.

In that span of time, BriseBois has seen the league completely transform from a management perspective. He once did a presentation while getting his MBA that compared the hockey operations departments of the Montreal Canadiens during the 1970s to the one in the early 2000s. The change was remarkable. It was nothing like it is now.

"Today, it's almost seventy people in hockey ops, it's incredible," BriseBois said. "When you factor in skating consultants, skill development people, player development people, sports psychologists, we have seven coaches in Tampa, we have four in Syracuse, there's so much."

It means, even as he taps into knowledge of those who came before him, his job now is completely different.

"You have to delegate. There's no other way," he said. "Your most important job is hiring really good people and then trusting them, delegating responsibilities, giving them support and resources to be successful. That's it."

That's it. BriseBois almost makes it sound simple. But to succeed over time in a league changing as rapidly as the NHL takes someone willing to evolve, someone willing to learn constantly. It also takes someone with core beliefs on management that are sharpened over time. To many of his admirers around the NHL, the leader who embodied that more than anyone in hockey was the person I would visit next.

CHAPTER 2

UNCOMPROMISING CORE BELIEFS

The only thing is you win. That's all I care about. I'm not going to apologize for it.

—Lou Lamoriello

I was waiting to be seated at an Italian restaurant with one of the most secretive men in sports. He's a guy who keeps things so tightly guarded that I was definitely uncomfortable when he got a call on the drive over and I could see who was calling on the car's giant dashboard screen.

We'd just entered Giulio Cesare on Ellison Avenue in Westbury, New York. When you walk into this place, you're surrounded by walls covered with framed photos of everyone famous who has passed through. Politicians, athletes, actors—most dressed formally and standing next to one of the owners, Giulio Donatich or Cesare Dundara.

"The gentleman who owns this place, if he's here, I think he's eighty-five years old. He works like he's twenty years old," said Lou Lamoriello, a winner of three Stanley Cups, who also happens to be the guy who picked this spot. He motioned to all the pictures surrounding us. *Look at these walls.* In the 1990s, the *New York Times* wrote about the charm of this Long Island spot, calling it "the kind of place where the owner is at the door greeting guests and hugging most of them; where large family groups gather for life's milestones and waiters cluster to sing 'Happy Birthday.'"

We weren't there to do that. We were continuing a conversation about team building and leadership that started in his office during the afternoon and now extended to dinner because when Lou Lamoriello asks if you're hungry, the answer is always yes.

The owner emerged and Lamoriello smiled.

"I was just talking about you. I wondered if you were here. Last time I came here, you must have gone on vacation."

"No vacation," he answered.

Lamoriello turned his attention to the decor surrounding us.

"He's got everything," Lamoriello said of the pictures on the wall. "You name it. I came here and he said, 'I've got the Devils here, too.' It was [Vladimir] Malakhov, because he lived on Long Island."

The owner got right to business.

"Two of you?"

"Just two. You've got this all set up for us? A private room."

He led us out of the entryway.

"I was worried about you," Lamoriello said to him as we made our way to the back room. "I came in here the other day and you weren't here."

"Sometimes I can't work too many hours, I take off lunch."

"I don't blame you."

Lamoriello ordered a glass of Chianti. I picked out a cabernet. I mean, at this point I was just following his lead.

"What fish came in today?" Lamoriello asked.

"Salmon. Swordfish. Red snapper."

Lamoriello turned to me as our host disappeared to grab the wine.

"He'll make anything for you. No matter what you want."

And then he paused.

"Eighty-five years old."

"Amazing."

It was September and Islanders camp was just about to open. Lamoriello was entering his fourth season running the Islanders, but had been running teams in the NHL since leaving Providence College in 1987. He was seventy-eight years old on the day we chatted, seven years junior to the owner of this restaurant, who clearly earned Lamoriello's respect with his longevity and work ethic. Lamoriello had the three Stanley Cup rings. He had a World Series ring from the Yankees in 2009. He put together a Team USA that had one of the unlikeliest championship runs in international hockey history in the 1996 World Cup. He was elected to the Hockey Hall of Fame in 2009. His place in the game is absolutely secure.

Still, he's working. In his case, there are no lunches off.

As we considered our fresh seafood options, Lamoriello was coming off guiding the Islanders to consecutive Eastern Conference Finals, running into the powerhouse Lightning twice and giving that team all it could handle before elimination.

Months later, he would fire the coach who led those teams to that accomplishment in the shocking dismissal of Barry Trotz. But really, it was only shocking if you don't know Lamoriello and how he operates. As much as anyone could know him. It's also the kind of move that makes Lamoriello one of the most fascinating managers in sports.

"Lou is one of the best at what he does that we've seen," said Rod Thorn, the basketball Hall of Famer who drafted Michael Jordan, helped put together the original Dream Team, and worked for Lamoriello with the NBA's New Jersey Nets. When Thorn said he's one of the best, he wasn't talking about Lamoriello in terms of running a hockey team. He was talking about running an organization, about winning.

"It's his ability to understand how you put a team together," Thorn said. "He is very adept at understanding what works, what doesn't, making decisions and not looking back."

But if we're being completely honest, those strategies and decisions can look puzzling from the outside. If you're analytically inclined or don't appreciate the kind of team-building rules Lamoriello implements without exception, you're probably suspicious of his methods. Some of it definitely looks dated from the outside, especially as the championships slowed later in his career. While I entered the conversation definitely respectful of all Lamoriello has accomplished, I had some questions about how it all fits into today's game.

I didn't understand the secrecy. I didn't understand the strict rules. The requirement to wear suits. The rules against taping up equipment. The elimination of individual personality. The player contracts sitting in a drawer and not getting announced until long after they're agreed to. The seemingly cold-blooded dismissal of coaches and deportment of players to Robidas Island.

And, of course, there are the rules around grooming. No long hair. No beards.

I definitely laughed in 2021 when he traded for Kyle Palmieri, a guy who I'm pretty sure came out of the womb with a full-scale beard. But the laugh was followed by questions: Why would a grown, millionaire athlete even tolerate these rules? And how are they even implemented?

In this case, on the night Palmieri was acquired, veteran defenseman Andy Greene got a call on FaceTime. Palmieri was in a Walgreens buying a razor for the first time since college. He didn't need anyone to tell him the Lamoriello rules. He knew what he had to do.

"He's twenty-six, twenty-seven years old, and he's like, 'What kind of razor do I buy?'" Greene said, laughing over the phone in retelling the story. Tom Fitzgerald, the Devils GM who traded Palmieri, asked him to text a picture on the night he shaved. This was a massive trade and the immediate focus was as much on the grooming as it was the deal.

"Everyone but Lou mentioned the shaving thing," Palmieri said.

This is how it goes.

I started the trip to Long Island with so many questions. And when he didn't provide the answers, I reached out to those who know him best to try and get them.

"Everything he did," Randy McKay, who won two Stanley Cups playing for Lamoriello, would explain later, "there was a purpose for. There was a reason.

"It was all about winning."

Seven months after leading the University of Georgia football team to the 2023 national championship, Bulldogs head coach

Kirby Smart was back in his office. He was going through his desk when he spotted a Post-it note stuck behind the chair. It had a message he would share at the podium during SEC Media Days the following summer.

"There's tons of books written on great leaders and leadership. What you won't see, what you will never see is people talking about the costs associated with leadership," he said.

Watching this clip, I thought of Lamoriello. In spending time with him, in talking to those who know him best, with those who were fired by him, traded by him, fought with him over contracts—there was always a price for Lamoriello to pay. Often at the cost of a public image he wasn't willing to correct.

"Great leaders are willing to accept those costs," Smart said. "Number one, you will have to make hard decisions that negatively affect people you care about. Number two, you will be disliked despite your best attempt to do the best for the most. Number three, you will be misunderstood and won't always have the opportunity to defend yourself."

Lamoriello certainly doesn't need defending or even seem to want defending.

But on a September afternoon that spilled into an evening Italian meal, he seemed willing to be understood. You hear the stories. Of a fiery Lamoriello putting someone in their place. Or how he's *everywhere*. All the time. His former coach Jacques Lemaire told a story about how Lamoriello didn't want the coaching staff drinking on the road around the players. They were at a hotel and Lemaire knew the manager, so he asked him to grab a few beers and set up a hidden spot by the kitchen.

"We're sitting there, fifteen to twenty minutes later, and who comes in? Lou. We were like, 'How the hell did he find us?' We laughed, that was so funny. We thought we had him. That's amazing," Lemaire said. "He's looking around all the time. He doesn't miss a practice. He's the first at the arena. . . . He rarely misses a game on the road except when he has an NHL meeting. That's his life: to be around the team and know what's going on."

Knowing this, knowing the work he puts in, I probably over-prepared for our conversation. I didn't shave, but I definitely thought about it. But the reality is, the Lou Lamoriello I met is one who has mellowed with time.

"We all change," Lemaire said. "Lately, the last eight years, he's never been upset. . . . If I look at the past, twenty years ago and the team would lose four or five games, then his language would be crisp, he would be not as peaceful. I think that's maturity or age. We're all like that."

The demeanor might be softer, but the belief system is very much intact.

"He still has the same philosophy that he had in the past when he talks to me," Lemaire said. "It's the exact same thing he believes. He won with that. He believes he can win again with the discipline, the work, all the elements that are part of him."

And any nerves I might have had about him were lifted the moment I walked into his office, with him sitting at his desk.

"Welcome to the Firm," he said.

Then he let out a laugh.

It was a nod to the book by John Grisham and movie with Tom Cruise about a law firm that worked with the mob and killed anyone who threatened to reveal the truth. It's also what players once secretly called playing for a Lamoriello team.

"That was us," McKay said. "Once you're in the Firm, there's no fucking getting out on your own. We started calling us the Firm. We used to keep it quiet, we thought."

They kept it quiet until Michael Farber referenced it in a 1999 *Sports Illustrated* story about the Devils, and if Lamoriello was mad about it at the time, he seemed to enjoy it now. He also got at the age issue immediately. As we sat down to chat, he looked over at Islanders communications executive Kimber Auerbach, who took a seat nearby as the conversation began.

"By the way, this is like the United States, where people are afraid of what Biden might say," Lamoriello said, and then laughed again.

To really attempt to understand Lamoriello is to first break the assumption he is part of hockey's old guard. It's an easy assumption to make. In a sports landscape where teams are looking for the next brilliant young executive to run a team, Lamoriello is old. He runs a hockey organization. He's been around the sport for decades. It definitely *feels* like old guard. But he entered the NHL as an outsider. And there was a time, decades ago, when he was the youngest at everything he did. He's a lifetime learner. He's always looking for an edge. He's always looking at what's next. He has an insatiable thirst for knowledge, as indicated by the shelf of books behind him loaded up with wisdom from finance to football. Or the video we'd watch later together. This got its genesis because he was always very young at whatever he took on.

"You can't tell that today," he joked.

But it definitely shapes him.

He graduated high school at sixteen. He was out of college at twenty.

"I always sort of respected that I was younger and I was more of a sponge," he said. And it was in those formative years when his ideas of how to run a team took shape.

He played hockey at Providence, and one of the coaches there was named Tom Eccleston. Eccleston had professors watch games and track stats in a way no other coaches did in those days.

"He was ahead of his time," Lamoriello said, settling in and sharing some of his past. "They would keep all these statistics of the game. How many passes we made. How many shots we took. We'd get a report card after the game. It used to bug a lot of people, but I was intrigued by it. You'd compete against yourself. If you had a couple bad passes, the next night you didn't want that."

Everything was tracked. Everything was accounted for. Nothing was missed.

In baseball, it was a coach named Alex Nahigian who left a lifelong impression. Nahigian played for Jack Barry, whose baseball lineage went back to Connie Mack and winning the World Series three times with the Philadelphia Athletics starting in 1910. Nahigian posted an .806 winning percentage as a college baseball coach. Baseball, as it would turn out, would end up influencing Lamoriello in a serious way. Really, every sport would play a part in shaping his philosophies. In talking to Lamoriello, there are casual firsthand references to the Montreal Canadiens, Green Bay Packers, New York Yankees, and Boston Celtics. And also Bruce Springsteen. And *The Sopranos*.

He's seen a lot.

It was Nahigian's black-and-white approach to communication that made the biggest impression, a style of communication that went back to Connie Mack and continues with Lamoriello.

"You knew where you stood every second," Lamoriello said.

But perhaps the greatest incubator of leadership during that era was the Providence athletic department while Lamoriello was running it. Lamoriello hired Rick Pitino to coach the basketball team and the staff included Jeff Van Gundy, Stu Jackson, and Herb Sendek. There was a kid on the team knocking down three-pointers at a record pace named Billy Donovan. Pitino would eventually win a national championship with Kentucky and was the first coach to lead three different teams to the Final Four. Donovan would win two national championships as men's basketball head coach of the Florida Gators. The others all would go on to lead college programs or NBA teams.

Lamoriello got an up-close look at how great coaches got the most out of every situation. He observed the different strategies that led to success.

"It was an education process that was going on that I never knew," he said.

The common thread that a Lamoriello-led athletics department demanded was that everyone put in the work. Donovan can still rattle off the Providence basketball practice schedule from those days. After an early-morning class, the team had an hour of skill development on the basketball court. Then another class. Then a practice that stretched nearly three hours. That was followed by a study hall after dinner and then back to the gym for scouting reports and free-throw shooting. On Saturdays there were double practice sessions and on Sunday triple sessions.

"If you're the [athletic director] and you're seeing that, you could very easily say, 'This is too much, you can't be doing this,'" Donovan said of how the department was run under Lamoriello. "But you're around all these guys that were passionate about it. Nonstop. You realized if you wanted to be good at something, this is what you had to put into it. Coach Lamoriello was in line with that. . . . He was always there. It wasn't like you were there and his car wasn't there. It all started from a premise of work. What wins in hockey, wins in basketball. It's the same that it was sixty years ago. The things that go into winning just don't change."

It's the willingness to put in the time. This group believed it.

"People want to think there's this illusion of choice. 'I want to be successful, but I don't want to put the work into what it takes,'" Donovan said. "Winning is not a buffet line."

On the basketball court, Donovan explained, winning games comes from taking a charge or boxing out or getting back in transition on defense. In hockey, it's blocking a shot, going into the corner to win a battle. Every sport has its examples.

"If you're not willing to work and invest in the things it takes to win, you're not serious about it," he said. "I respect what the Miami Heat say a lot of times. 'This is not for everybody and everybody is not for us.' There's a lot of truth to that. There's a line that gets drawn of the things you have to do. There are certain guys that will go above that line."

Those are the players Lamoriello sets out to find when building his teams. And then he does everything in his power to remove every possible distraction. And whatever it takes to get an edge.

———

If the last several years in hockey have taught us anything, it's that we don't truly know anybody. We only know the version of reality that is presented to the world and the truths that are revealed over time. I thought about that a lot while working on this book.

And especially this portion because Lou Lamoriello is

complicated. Brian Burke, who played for him at Providence and might be as close to him as anybody in hockey, captured it well in his book, *Burke's Law*.

> No one has been more influential in my professional life. I owe him a lot. He got me through four years of college and got me a scholarship to pay for my education. He's the only reason I went to law school. I have learned so much from him.
>
> All in all, I ought to know Lou better than just about anyone outside of his immediate family. But the fact is, while I like him and respect him immensely, I don't really know him. If someone asked me if I was close to Lou the person, my answer would have to be no. He's as much of an enigma to me as he is to everyone else.

That may be true, but so is the intense loyalty he's earned over the years by others who believe they know him well. Even those who have been fired by him. Or those who would follow him anywhere. Maybe that's part of the enigma. To some he's unknowable, to others it's pretty simple.

"He creates an environment where you're a part of it and you go to war for him," said Steve Pellegrini, who left the NHL to work with Lamoriello and the Devils in 2006 and then again with the New York Islanders. But how? That's what I was really interested in. Pellegrini shared one small story that he felt captured it. One afternoon, shortly after he was hired in New Jersey, Pellegrini was at a restaurant by a lake, having lunch with his dad.

Lamoriello called and Pellegrini mentioned he was with his father.

"Let me talk to him," Lamoriello said.

Pellegrini handed over the phone. At this point, Lamoriello had already reached a bit of a mythical status in the game with his Stanley Cups and very specific methods to build culture, but during this moment he was just a boss saying great things about one of his employees to their dad. They spoke for twenty minutes.

The next week a box full of Devils merchandise showed up at Pellegrini's dad's house. Lamoriello had sent it. When Pellegrini had a death in the family, there weren't just flowers from the team. There were two huge bouquets—one from the team, the other from Lamoriello. Lamoriello also took care of food and drinks. There were appetizers and wine to let the family know that he was there in full support during the toughest times.

"He talks about treating players as the player and the person. It's the same thing with his employees," Pellegrini said. "The stuff he's done for my family over the years has been unbelievable."

Mike "Doc" Emrick was a broadcaster of Devils games for years. In the fall of 2003, the Yankees were playing the Marlins in the World Series and Emrick's brother, Dan, a die-hard baseball fan, was visiting from Indiana with a teaching colleague. Emrick asked Lamoriello, who was on the Yankees board, if there was any shot at getting his brother World Series tickets. Lamoriello told him to stop by the Yankees sales window. The seats waiting, to a clinching World Series game, were five rows behind the Marlins dugout. In Emrick's mind, that was way more than he expected, but Lamoriello followed it up with another question.

"How long are they in town? See if they can go to lunch with me."

Lamoriello picked them up and took them to an Italian restaurant. Again, there's a private room waiting.

"We walk in and my brother nudges me," Emrick said. "You see who that is?"

Yankees Hall of Famer Yogi Berra was waiting for them. Lamoriello had set it all up. "That's what he does," Emrick said in explaining why people are so loyal to Lamoriello. "He works dawn to dusk and he takes care of people. . . . He was always there for us."

Scott Gomez played more than one thousand NHL games, including his first seven seasons playing for Lamoriello, and might have spent more time in his office for disciplinary reasons than any other player. He also went to arbitration against Lamoriello during a contract dispute. Twice. An arbitration case may be the ultimate test of a relationship between a player and a team, and generally, the two sides don't survive it. Gomez remembered sitting through the first one and wanting to crawl over the table to take a swing at Lamoriello.

"That's a long hour," Gomez said. "You also learn from Lou, this is a business. He's the master at it."

The second case was only thirty minutes of arguments for each side, but just as painful. Nobody wants to hear that they're not worth what they think they are. After the second session wrapped, Gomez ran into Lamoriello in the bathroom. Tension was still high, at least from Gomez's point of view. Lamoriello removed the tension immediately.

"Scotty, this is the bad side," he said calmly. "How are you getting home?"

It was a Saturday. Gomez had an eight o'clock flight out of Toronto the next morning. He started thinking of the long line through customs. The early wake-up call. None of it sounded great.

"You want to go with me? I have a plane," Lamoriello offered. "Just come home now."

A few minutes later, they're sharing a cab, heading back to New Jersey together.

Just come home now.

"That's how he was," Gomez said. "If I ever got in serious trouble, if something happened, Lou would be the first call I'd ever make. Over my parents. That's the respect and love I have."

Sitting in Lamoriello's office with the Islanders, I asked him about these stories. How much of this is intentional, to get players and staff on his side in the name of building a culture? He turned the question back at me. He'd do this a lot in our conversations.

"When you have a family and you see somebody who is in a position capable of doing something and they send something to a loved one of your own, doesn't that have a great impression?"

He started sharing stories of people in hockey who had reached out to his son. Or of the time the Islanders were in Raleigh and his daughter stopped by to visit the Islanders after the game and he spotted Barry Trotz spending a few minutes saying hello.

"Why don't we do more of this?" Lamoriello asked. "Sometimes you're so mad at yourself because your mind is different at a different time and you might be negligent about doing that. You might say those are the things that bother you the most."

If he's doing it, he added, he's doing these things only to build relationships. When the marketing team tries to force it, he declines, which creates strain for those looking to promote the game outside of hockey operations. He said he's fought those battles over the years—the kind of sincere connections you make to build a team versus those done only for publicity. He has no time for moments he doesn't view as genuine.

"You do it only because of that person, not because you want somebody to know it," he said. "Everybody wants to show the nice things. I want things done because it's the right thing, because it's coming from here."

He tapped his chest.

When I sent the email, I honestly didn't expect an answer. Viacheslav Fetisov is a member of the Russian parliament, and when the request to chat was made, his country was in the middle of a war with Ukraine. He had sanctions levied against him by the United States and its allies because of the invasion of Ukraine. But before he became a political leader in Russia, Fetisov was the best example of the extremes Lamoriello went to in order to give his team an edge. Sometimes those extremes mean flying the team bus driver to road games during the playoffs so a familiar person is transporting his players to the rink at all times. Sometimes they mean firing someone because they're late. Sometimes they mean traveling to Russia and putting your life on the line to try and return with a defenseman known as Slava, who is one of the best players in the world not playing in the NHL.

As told in the *Red Army* documentary, Fetisov was promised that he'd be able to go to the NHL and play for Lamoriello's New Jersey Devils if he won a gold medal in the 1988 Winter Olympics. He upheld his end of the deal, and shortly after, he was called into a meeting with the head of sports in Russia and legendary coach Viktor Tikhonov, who let him know he couldn't go.

The Soviet team traveled to the United States to play an exhibition game against the New Jersey Devils, a team that had an offer on the table for Fetisov to play one season. The Red Army steamrolled the Devils, and Fetisov was taken on a tour of New York by Lamoriello. During that tour, Lamoriello told Fetisov he believed the Soviets were never going to let him leave.

You should stay here.

In the documentary, Fetisov shared his response to Lamoriello.

"No," he said. "I cannot run away from my country. I cannot do something illegal."

But in a press conference in Moscow, he announced that he would never play for Tikhonov again because he felt cheated. That public declaration froze Fetisov out of every sports facility in Russia. People he knew cut off communication. He said he was followed, his conversations were tracked. His mother was threatened. One night in Kiev, Fetisov was handcuffed, beaten, and handed off to Tikhonov at 4 a.m. The message from Tikhonov: don't let him out of the country. Fetisov's teammates publicly stood up for him on television. They threatened to stop playing. Then Alexander Mogilny defected to join the Buffalo Sabres. Then Igor Larionov joined the Vancouver Canucks.

As this was happening, Fetisov was negotiating with the Soviet Defense Ministry over how much of his NHL salary he'd get to keep and how much he'd have to give them. These negotiations eventually led to Fetisov telling the second most powerful man in Russia: *Release me from the army.*

Ultimately, he was granted a working visa to play in the United States.

People may never understand what Lamoriello did behind the

scenes while all this was happening to add the defenseman to his roster.

"We went through a lot," Lamoriello said in his office. "I'd rather have him tell you."

So the email request was sent to Fetisov in Russia. Two weeks later came the reply.

"Hi Craig. [I'd] like to do it."

During his pursuit of Fetisov, who was drafted a second time by the Devils in the eighth round of the 1983 draft, Lamoriello said he hired a secretary whose primary responsibility was to call Fetisov over and over again in an attempt to connect over the phone. Lamoriello enlisted the help of chess player Garry Kasparov, who he said was instrumental in getting Fetisov over. He connected with John Whitehead, the U.S. deputy secretary of state under Ronald Reagan. He went to the Russian embassy in Washington several times.

Years later, Lamoriello and Fetisov would have a Christmas dinner together in New Jersey where Fetisov let him know just how much danger he put himself in during this pursuit.

"I said, 'Lou, you know what I figured out—you coming to Russia in 1988, we got no visa, you crossed the border without permission, you can be lost in my country because you have no official entrance,'" Fetisov said during the phone call from Moscow.

You can be lost is quite the phrase.

With Kasparov's help, Lamoriello entered Russia through Finland and made arrangements to do it without a formal entry because he didn't want Russian officials to know he was in the country to sign their star player. The problem, Lamoriello would explain years later, is that if nobody knows you went into the country, nobody would know you never made it out.

"It was scary what I explained to him," Fetisov said. "I know from the officials the situation. He came because he's a good guy."

That was part of it.

"I needed a defenseman," Lamoriello said.

And he also didn't realize just how much danger he was in at the time, not until Fetisov filled in more details over that Christmas dinner. He still doesn't like to think about it too much.

"Today, I look back and think I was out of my mind," Lamoriello said.

Risking his life to add a defenseman to the roster in order to try and prop up a bad team is one thing. But to succeed in doing it and then trade him a few years later? That's pure Lamoriello. As it would turn out, Fetisov wasn't a great fit for that Devils team. There was an adjustment in playing styles, and Russians coming over at that time were viewed as people taking jobs from the good North American boys. Fetisov said many of his Devils teammates didn't want him there.

"I feel that hate from my teammates when I came," Fetisov said. "Lou was the biggest ambassador. He feels we need to communicate, play for one team, for the one goal."

And when it didn't work? Lamoriello pulled the plug. On April 3, 1995, he sent the thirty-six-year-old Fetisov to the Detroit Red Wings for a third-round pick. Fetisov would go on to form the famed Russian Five in Detroit under Scotty Bowman, winning back-to-back Stanley Cups in 1997 and 1998. When Fetisov retired after that second Stanley Cup, it was Lamoriello who convinced him to come back to New Jersey as an assistant coach.

That offer led to another Stanley Cup for Fetisov, this one in 2000 with the Devils.

"He was pushing me and pushing me. He called me almost

every day. 'You should become a coach. You should come here. You're going to be successful,'" Fetisov said. "That was one of my best four years was working for the organization with Larry Robinson and Lou Lamoriello—we built one of the [most] creative hockey teams in the history of the NHL. Part of my success story over there."

Sounds great. And then what happened?

"He fired us," Fetisov said.

Less than two years after leading the Devils to a Stanley Cup, Robinson and his staff were fired and replaced by disciplinarian Kevin Constantine. After the move, Fetisov said Lamoriello met him in a parking lot in New Jersey and told him that his future was back in Russia. He saw a future for Fetisov where he could run the sport in his home country. He planted the seed in Fetisov's head that he could have great success taking a leadership role in returning home. The story between Fetisov and Lamoriello is one that captures nearly every angle of Lamoriello's leadership. His relentless pursuit of Fetisov. Trading him when it wasn't working. Bringing him back. Winning a Stanley Cup. Firing him when the standard wasn't maintained. Giving him the advice that would end up setting up the rest of his life.

"He should be a visionary," Fetisov said. "Sometimes he's very tough, because he's supposed to be. Sometimes he's very sensitive. Many times he's right."

There was a black binder on Lamoriello's desk and he flipped to a printout in protective plastic that read in typed and underlined all caps: BASIC RULES. Lamoriello said he reads these reminders every day.

Do what's right

Have honest, open, timely communication

Say what you mean and do what you say

Work as a team. There is no "I" in We

Respect each Individual

Treat others as you would like to be treated

Be the best at what you do

Have a purpose in every action

Do it now!

"You know what it does? It keeps you on track," Lamoriello said. "It's easy to sometimes get a little soft, a little weak. Or you're tired. You have to be careful. It's tough to explain. . . . It's easy, you can get worn a little. You have to be careful."

Next to the binder was a book by former Green Bay Packers coach Vince Lombardi that he'd read so many times the pages were falling out. Literally. I walked over to his desk to take a look and I didn't even want to touch it because he said he wasn't sure he could buy a replacement.

The page that was sitting open on his desk read: "I firmly believe that any man's finest hour—his greatest fulfillment to all he holds dear—is that moment when he has worked his heart out in a good cause and lies exhausted on the field of battle—victorious."

Lamoriello shared a story about Lombardi that stuck with him. How Lombardi had Bart Starr walk the entire Packers team out of a restaurant in the South because they wouldn't serve the entire team. These stories had an impact on him. As did the stories he learned firsthand from guys like Mike Krzyzewski, Bill Parcells, and Tom Landry when they'd pass through town.

"In that era, I was coming up and coaching in college and doing all the things that you're learning every day—you're trying to pick up whatever you can pick up. Whenever these big-time coaches would come to Providence, you're sitting here saying, 'Invite me to lunch.' Then you get some of their stories. Some of the things they went through."

That approach to learning left its impression on the young guard Billy Donovan. Years later, when he started coaching, he'd spend time with coaches in other sports to try and pick up anything that might help him win, just like he learned from Lamoriello. One year, after getting knocked out of the NCAA tournament in the early round with what he believed were good players at Florida, Donovan spent time with Patriots coach Bill Belichick. Belichick asked him: What kind of identity do you want for your team? Donovan considered the question for a moment and then answered. He wanted his group to be tough mentally and physically. He wanted a team with high IQ.

"That's exactly what we want with the Patriots," he remembered Belichick answering. "No difference. . . . Now start recruiting *those* guys. Start getting *those* guys. You want discipline and toughness? Go recruit it. You want IQ? Go recruit it."

Like Donovan, Lamoriello is a great listener. He doesn't miss a thing. Even as I was trying to pry as much information as possible from Lamoriello during our conversation, he'd ask questions about situations I was dealing with. Managing writers. Making decisions at *The Athletic*. He pieced together that I was putting off a major decision, even without knowing the details, and he pushed me to face it and deal with it in the moment.

"The thing you always remember when you go through that—the president of the United States or the top military person goes through that every day," Lamoriello said. "You've got to get over the hump. You can't worry about the noise. You can't worry about the personal feelings."

He also advised that the people who work in an organization, those doing a great job, are always watching the person in charge to see if they'll make the tough decision.

"The people who are pushing to get better are feeling, 'Are we going to get better?'" Lamoriello said. "It's all relevant. Your job is relevant to mine. It's all relevant when it comes down to certain systemic parts of it."

We started talking about books. Of course he's got all the John Wooden books at home. And he loves Bill Russell's book. And while conversations through the years with legends passing through New York might have shaped him in his younger days, he's still looking to add to them. He started flipping through Tim Ferriss's book *Tribe of Mentors*, which has insight from people like poker star Annie Duke, actor/investor Ashton Kutcher, and Olympian Dara Torres, among many, many others. He once recommended it to Islanders forward Mathew Barzal to read.

He's a fan of Ryan Holiday and his consumable stoicism. If he can find any morsel of information that can help him get better, he'll use it. Shortly before I showed up at his office, he was sent a clip of Harold Reynolds interviewing Derek Jeter, reminiscing about his career with the Yankees. He wanted to share it.

"You've got time?"

I got up to watch the clip as it was pulled up on a phone and Jeter started talking.

"Because of the rules we have in New York, I'd never gone

a day without shaving. Rules. Rules. You've got to have rules. It teaches you discipline," Jeter began.

No wonder Lamoriello loved this video.

"Rules. Discipline. How much did that play into your success?" Reynolds asked.

"It's all discipline. You know what I mean? You have to have routine. I had a ritual. . . . My biggest fear in life is to be unprepared."

Jeter talked about winning early in his career and the impact it made on him. Then he started talking as if he was channeling Lamoriello.

"I came up in a culture, if you didn't do your job . . . you would get someone else. Without hesitation. We were always looking over our shoulder."

"Did that help you on the road to greatness though?"

"Yeah, you're never happy. I think that's how I'm built anyway. You're never happy with what you've done. Forget it, that's over with. Done. You celebrate for a week or two and you move to what's next."

For Lamoriello, those moments of celebration look different than those of the players. When his teams win the Stanley Cup, he prefers to stay in the background. In 2000, after the Devils beat the Dallas Stars to win the Stanley Cup, he and his coach, Larry Robinson, hailed a cab and went to the hospital to visit Petr Sykora, who had been hospitalized following a hit to the head from Dallas's Derian Hatcher. After that visit, they skipped the celebration with the players and instead found two chairs near the team bus and sat outside enjoying the moment. Mostly, they enjoyed watching others enjoy the moment.

"There is no greater satisfaction to seeing that. That's what

UNCOMPROMISING CORE BELIEFS

you want—people who haven't experienced that, to experience it," Lamoriello said. "There's nothing like it."

"Lou and I sat there reminiscing about the year and the stuff that went on throughout the year," Robinson said. "It was a cool moment. Probably the best time. There's nobody else around. You have just you and your thoughts and you're with somebody you truly enjoy being around. I love Lou like he's my dad."

Another one of those moments for Lamoriello came with a different coach. In 2010, he got a call from Line Burns, wife of his old coach and friend Pat Burns. Burns was in hospice care and Lamoriello dropped everything he was doing to visit.

Burns was in the final stages of his fight with cancer. Everything and everybody had been cleared out of the room when Lamoriello arrived. It was just Burns in bed next to a photo.

"He couldn't even speak," Lamoriello said. "It was a picture of the Stanley Cup. He grabbed my hand.

"That's what makes it all worthwhile."

<hr>

By the time we got around to talking about the shaving rule, I suspected how he'd answer. Shaving was about becoming a group of one, right down to how players on the team start the day. Jeter hinted at it. Lamoriello expanded on it.

"Yeah. It's 'We're one,'" Lamoriello said. "And every day, you wake up in the morning, the first thing you do is you either swear at me or you say, 'I'm an Islander.' Or 'I'm a Maple Leaf.' Or 'I'm a Devil.' It's a pride thing. Players, after they've been around, it's automatic."

Lamoriello had recently visited Camp Pendleton, one of the

largest Marine Corps bases in the United States, and he was re-minded again why this rule existed.

"Think about the most important people in the world, the people who protect us," Lamoriello said. "They bring people in, from any denomination. . . . People who have a lot of money, people who don't have a dime. They're all together. The first thing they do is they get a common denominator, to make them all the same the best way they can. . . . You try and get a group together. That's what it's all about."

To be clear, not every player is on board with this rule. When I raised the rule with NHL veteran Nick Foligno, who has played most of his career with a face full of hair, he shot it down immediately.

"I can't stand it. I have a ton of respect for Lou, but I don't believe in that. I love the fact that there's different characters in the room. . . . I get what Lou is trying to do. I think that is dangerous sometimes."

Foligno believes that players being allowed to express themselves helps them play at their best. He also believes it's the best thing for the sport if players are allowed to show individuality.

"At the end of the day, are you going to go to battle for your team? I don't care what you look like or what you're into. If you care about the team, that's all I care about," he said.

The criticism of Lamoriello has gone beyond the grooming debate. In 2019, former New Jersey Devil Mike Peluso filed a lawsuit against the Devils that named Lou Lamoriello and claimed that doctors hid the extent of his injuries as a fighter that led to nine seizures and early-onset dementia. After Lamoriello exiled Neal Broten before trading him to the Los Angeles Kings in 1996, Broten let his feelings be known in that *Sports Illustrated* story by Michael Farber.

"I mean, he's just a cruel person," Broten said. "I don't think I've met one person who likes him. I know I don't. How do you sleep at night treating people like that?"

I asked him about Broten.

"Without him, we don't win the '95 Cup. By the way, I'm sure he's still sour today," Lamoriello answered. "But you make those decisions. I regret a couple of things I've done, certain situations I might have been able to handle more discreetly. . . . Maybe I could have handled it better up to that point. Maybe I could have helped this out a little more. Maybe I could have done something. When you go to there, you don't look back. What you do do is some self-evaluation and you don't apologize for this. To yourself, you say, 'What can I do so that I do better next time?'"

Lamoriello's rigid ways filter right down to how he deals with the media. He's extremely protective of information. He rarely elaborates on why he makes the moves he does. I realize I'm biased, but I think this hurts the game. I think a sport like hockey, fighting for attention in a crowded landscape, benefits from transparency. When I suggested to him that there's value in communicating his thought process through the media to his fan base, he disagreed.

"Why should I explain what's in my head?"

To build the sport? To educate the fans?

"Winning heals everything," Lamoriello said. "I don't care how much I sit and tell you. . . . The only thing is you win. That's all I care about. I'm not going to apologize for it."

When Bill Guerin played for Lamoriello, they definitely didn't always agree. They had a dispute over a contract that eventually led to Guerin asking to be traded. But he thinks back to Lamoriello's obsession over details in the name of winning and really

believes it worked. In 1995, when the Devils played the Detroit
Red Wings in the Stanley Cup Final, the team stayed together
in a hotel both on the road and at home. At home, everybody—
players, management, coaches, trainers—ate dinners together at
a place called Bareli's. One night the team was enjoying the traditional meal together and a player from the Red Wings walked in.

"He was on his own. We were with teammates," Guerin said.
"And that was, to me, that was an edge. You might not think it's a
big thing, but it was. I think that player was shocked to see us and
I don't think he stayed."

Running his own team, Guerin sees Lamoriello in the way he
handles things. If the plane leaves at two, the door is shutting at
one forty-five and the team is leaving regardless of who might not
be on the flight. He's left players behind who were late for the bus.

"We still wear ties to games. Small stuff like that," Guerin
said. "Even if you're in the locker room you don't wear hats at the
table. . . . It's a little corny maybe, but I think it makes a difference. Have good manners. Carry yourself like a professional and
you'll play like a professional."

Guerin likened it to turning into your dad. Old sayings start
to come out. No hats at the dinner table. Ties to the game.

"When I grew up and became a GM, there are a lot of things
from Lou I turned into," he said. "I think it's a good thing."

Bobby Holik hasn't played an NHL game since 2009, but he
still wakes up every morning at five o'clock. He reads. He gets
dressed. He exercises. When I called him in Montana, he wasn't
coaching hockey, he was coaching a 4-H trapshooting club. And
even for that he was putting on pressed pants and a clean shirt.

"It's about respecting what I do. It's not about me," Holik said.
"By getting ready, you're respecting what you're going to do."

He thinks back to the late nights flying back to New Jersey after road trips and noticing Lamoriello showing up first the next day in a jacket and a tie. It set the tone. After a recent 4-H competition, Holik gathered the kids around him before the winners were named. He told them that it wasn't about the results. It was about how they prepared. It was the effort they put in. The focus and respect they gave the task in front of them. Turns out, if that's the approach, winning often follows.

In the conversation with Holik, I made the mistake of calling Lamoriello's approach an obsession.

"It's not obsession, it's a way of doing things," Holik said. "It's a way of life. Discipline. Structure. Work ethic. Sacrifice. Every day—whether you play hockey or anything—you stay with those principles and values and the consistency is going to put you over the top."

Lamoriello's impact on his former players was clear. It's long-lasting, even if they resisted it at first. And if they resisted, the person I'd sit down with next could certainly relate.

CHAPTER 3

THE EDUCATION OF EXPERIENCE

If you really want to do something great, you're going to have to stare down immense doubt and challenge and you're going to have to make big decisions.

—**Kyle Dubas**

So much had changed in the two years since Kyle Dubas and I sat in this place. Dubas, for one, was no longer the general manager of the team he was when we chatted. When we met here, he was running the Toronto Maple Leafs. Two years later, he was trying to help Sidney Crosby win another Stanley Cup as the president and general manager of the Pittsburgh Penguins after being replaced in Toronto by Brad Treliving in a very public and slightly bizarre regime change.

But in Horizon Books, two years after we chatted, it felt like time had stood still.

This bookstore, in the northern Michigan resort town of Traverse City, is glorious in the way that all bookstores are glorious. It has quirks that make it one of a kind. This one is two stories of yellowish wooden shelves sitting on well-worn carpet. It doesn't have a massive assortment of books, but each topic has a curated selection of just the right choices for this corner of the world. I stopped by the hockey section and there were books on Red Wings legend Nicklas Lidstrom, the Russian Five, and the 1980 U.S. gold medal Olympic team. Someone here definitely knew their audience. I walked over to where Dubas and I first chatted, and the worn wooden chairs and maroon table where we sat had been moved to an adjacent window overlooking a canal and the nearby bay. The place has a distinct smell to it. Breathe it in and there's a hint of Sunday school church basement mixed with printer paper. I could stay there all day.

The first time we met, the Maple Leafs prospects in town had testing starting at 7:30 a.m. We agreed to meet at the bookstore after it wrapped. I was there early, grabbing a coffee and sitting in the same exact spot where I once interviewed Crosby by phone because it was the best place in this small town to get cell reception. I never imagined one day Dubas and Crosby would be so connected.

I sent a text, offering to grab him a coffee.

"On my way," he responded, accepting the offer for coffee with the request for a small bit of milk.

Dubas entered the front door wearing a black Puma jacket with the Premier League's Manchester City logo on the front and a Toronto Blue Jays hat. Because of the demands on his time as the general manager of the Maple Leafs, I was always conscious of giving him his space. But when we talk, it tends to be an easy conversation. We have shared interests, like enjoying the simplicity of walking up and down the aisles of a bookstore or trying to find a good local restaurant on the road. We both grew up Detroit Lions fans, which comes with its own special neurosis. But mostly, I connect with his curiosity. He genuinely wants to learn how things work in order to make himself better at what he does. His close friend Chris Armstrong, a golf agent at Creative Artists Agency, has seen that curiosity up close. One of Armstrong's clients, golf instructor Sean Foley, was speaking at the Sloan Sports Analytics Conference in Boston. Armstrong, Foley, and Dubas ended up in the same bar after a day full of panels and networking. That shared curiosity and eagerness to find ways to improve led to a quick connection. The three started a running text chain, one focused on how to get the best out of athletes. What works for motivating golfers often works for motivating hockey players.

"We have this appetite to consume as much information as possible," said Armstrong when we chatted. "The beauty of that is he does it in a structured fashion. He has a good understanding of his core principles and then he seeks information that expands his knowledge in those areas."

It's why I felt a bookstore was the perfect environment for us to chat. Dubas walked into Horizon and immediately started by asking about this book, the questions kicking in. He wanted to know how it went with Lou Lamoriello. He wanted to know who else I had talked to. I mentioned getting steamrolled in pickleball by Julien BriseBois and he wasn't surprised. I'm still not sure how to take that.

"He's good," Dubas said, adding that the two have grown close over the years as leaders of competing teams. "We played each other nine million times—Toronto and Tampa. So even though it's a rivalry, it's two guys who came in together."

The conversation shifted to Lamoriello. When Lamoriello

left the Maple Leafs there was a public narrative that suggested Dubas forced the issue in becoming the GM. At a minimum, I assumed there was tension between Dubas and Lamoriello. Only one of them could be the GM in Toronto for the long term and Dubas, at that moment, was the choice. Lamoriello was the first to shoot that down.

"Kyle is a tremendous kid," Lamoriello said. "I have tremendous respect for him. We had an exceptional relationship, today it's the same. We can separate—talking about family and talking about business. And I root for him. I'm his biggest fan and I think he knows that. And the world thought different."

At least I did.

"It was a strange situation," I answered. "He's the heir apparent. You're coming in as the guy who knows how to win. I don't know. It was an odd setup."

"It took a while . . ."

Lamoriello paused and changed direction.

"He could call me up any time of the night and day and I would be there. I'm sure the reverse is true," he said.

Maybe it is. But it was Lamoriello's initial answer that I found more interesting—it took a while. In the conversation with Dubas, he'd explain what that meant.

We strolled through the bookstore and passed by the psychology section. Dubas stopped. He pointed to a book by Daniel Kahneman, winner of the Nobel prize in economic sciences, called *Thinking, Fast and Slow*. It's a book about when we should trust our instincts and when we shouldn't. It's a deep dive into the systems that shape our decision-making. Every time someone points out how impactful it is for them, I'm reminded that I only got halfway through it.

"I think everyone who works in sports should read this book every year," Dubas said.

Then another book caught his eye. This one, I'd read all the way through. It was a book called *The Biggest Bluff*, written by Maria Konnikova, who went from never playing poker to learning from one of the best and becoming a pro. Poker is the subject, but it's really about learning about yourself.

"I think it's incredible," Dubas said.

He pulled another book off the shelf, this one called *Relentless: From Good to Great to Unstoppable*, by Tim S. Grover. Grover was a trainer for Michael Jordan and Kobe Bryant. Dubas read it while he was running the Soo Greyhounds. He said there was a point where the team was good, but just couldn't beat Connor McDavid. He was so moved by the advice from Grover that he gave everybody on the team a copy.

Another book ended up having an impact on him while running the Greyhounds. Around the time he was changing coaches in the Soo, he read the book *Daring Greatly* by Brené Brown, and inside the book was the quote from Teddy Roosevelt about the Man in the Arena. Growing up in Sault Ste. Marie, Dubas had never come across that passage, and when he did in Brown's book it ended up affecting his decision-making with the Greyhounds. He was facing a choice at head coach and was advised to be conservative in his hiring process, especially because of his age. He was told to find a veteran to stabilize the situation, since a mistake with a coaching hire at twenty-six years old might submarine his entire management career. He read this book and it inspired him to take the risk he felt was necessary in hiring Sheldon Keefe.

"It occurred to me, this whole view of how to operate and how to manage and how to do all that right? Vulnerability. The key thing was, if you really want to do something great, you're going to have to stare down immense doubt and challenge and you're going to have to make big decisions," Dubas said. "If I want to keep my job as long as possible, I could keep what we're doing, get to the end of the year, see if they'll keep me. I really believed in Sheldon, I had done as much homework as you possibly could on and off ice, the whole history part, and I really believed that, in terms of the way his teams played in Pembroke, the way he coached the team that we had, it would allow us both to achieve what we wanted."

It ended up being a smart hire, one that he'd make again in the NHL.

"That book was massive," he said of *Daring Greatly*'s influence of the Keefe hire.

We kept strolling through sections. He spotted *Atomic Habits* and mentioned that he got the entire Maple Leafs staff that book at one point. There was a book by Adam Grant, a professor of organizational psychology at the Wharton School, who Dubas has gotten to know through the years. It was a Grant book called *Originals* that Dubas read around the time he was being pursued by the Colorado Avalanche.

That book talks about the criticism nonconformists face when they try to do something new.

"When you believe in things different than conventional wisdom, you're going to take on a lot of criticism," Dubas said. "I've been lucky that I've found books at times when I've really needed them or they somehow find me."

But still, nothing beats real-life experience. And when Lamoriello joined the Maple Leafs organization, Dubas received a course worthy of an entire section of books.

———————

In April of 2015, Maple Leafs team president Brendan Shanahan fired general manager Dave Nonis after another disappointing season. It was announced that Dubas and Mark Hunter would share general manager responsibilities, and in a short period of time a lot was accomplished. Hunter focused on the upcoming draft, while Dubas dug into improving the roster. In May, the Maple Leafs hired coach Mike Babcock on an eight-year deal that altered the coaching landscape in the NHL. In June, the Maple Leafs drafted Mitch Marner, the second of the core four to join the franchise. In July, Phil Kessel was dealt to the Pittsburgh Penguins. The franchise was making massive moves during a time in which Dubas was sharing general manager duties. For an executive who still hadn't cracked thirty years old, it felt pretty great in the moment to be part of it.

"But looking back on it, it was very haphazard," Dubas said. "We needed Lou."

Shanahan felt the same way. At the end of July, the seventy-two-year-old Lamoriello accepted the job to replace Nonis as the general manager. It was a surprising hire on a lot of accounts. For one, he wasn't exactly coming off massive successes in his final few years running the Devils, despite having won three Stanley Cups and making two other trips to the Final. He was the team president in New Jersey, but new GM Ray Shero was building the roster.

"It was viewed as the fact that, the sun was setting, he was well into the back nine, and it was nearly over," Dubas said of the perception of Lamoriello at the time.

He also was taking a job where he didn't have complete control, something he generally demanded throughout his career. This setup was a departure from how Lamoriello generally demanded his front office be structured.

"But you don't let that get in the way. What you do is you try and adjust because you respect what you're trying to do," Lamoriello said. "It's nobody's fault. I didn't have that—what I have today. But I knew that, so it's no excuses or anything. But there's a difference. Every personality is different. There are some people who can do it differently. That's why I told George Steinbrenner, I have to be able to succeed or fail on me."

That wasn't the case in Toronto, but Lamoriello viewed the Maple Leafs job as a challenge. He had been given the opportunity to retire in New Jersey and was taken care of financially for life, but he still had that drive to win. He had his health. So he took the job, even if not having autonomy meant a different approach.

"How do I put it? When you don't have the autonomy one hundred percent, you're a little more hesitant than you should be," Lamoriello said. "That's all."

For Dubas, the addition of Lamoriello meant going from being in the room for massive decisions to clearing everything through a new boss. It was a dramatic change. There were moments when he wondered what exactly he'd gotten into in joining the Toronto front office. He left a job he loved as general manager of the Sault Ste. Marie Greyhounds of the Ontario Hockey League and it wasn't as easy a decision as it might have looked from the outside.

What ultimately convinced him to join the Maple Leafs was the promise that he'd be involved in everything. Under Lamoriello, he wasn't.

"That first year, Kyle got his hand slapped by Lou," said Dave Torrie, a longtime hockey scout and executive who was a mentor to Dubas. "Lou made him focus on certain things and tied his hands. What Lou was doing was testing this kid to see what he was made of."

Dubas was a rising star in hockey. But one thing that Torrie believes about Dubas is that his ego doesn't get in the way of progress. He remembered times when they worked together when Torrie was the general manager and Dubas was on his staff. Veteran scouts would walk in the room and Dubas knew everything about these scouts. He would recite players they drafted and then ask questions about the process. In a hockey world suspicious of youth, especially if youth comes citing analytics, Dubas won them over with humility and knowledge. Torrie believes that is how it played out with Lamoriello. Dubas's ego took a back seat.

"Instead of being upset and pouting, he did what Lou told him to do," Torrie said. "This is one of the most respected men in hockey. I think Kyle had to earn Lou's respect. I think he did."

Lamoriello assigned Dubas's responsibilities. He would be the general manager of the AHL's Toronto Marlies, he would have research and development responsibilities and be the conduit between the organization and the analytics department. There are two ways to look at that. He now had a clearly defined role or he was being limited under a controlling new boss. If Dubas felt limited, time adjusted his perspective.

"It was exactly what I needed," Dubas said. "The first year it was spread yourself extraordinarily thin, and in the second year, it was Lou saying, 'These are the three areas I want you to manage and work on and I'll ask you whatever I need.' . . . In the beginning, I was like, 'This is exactly what everybody said not to do when you're deciding to leave' and then, I don't know why, but I trusted he would have my best interests in the long run."

When Dubas took over for Lamoriello as Toronto's GM in 2018 he had changed as a leader. The Lamoriello influence was clear, from how Dubas approached media to his opinion on team rules. Had you asked Dubas before he worked under Lamoriello about things like a dress code or whether or not a player should be allowed long hair, he would have adhered to the Joe Maddon dress code: if you look hot, wear it.

That changed.

"I think the players need to feel that the players are going to their job," Dubas said. "If you work at Horizon bookstore, you probably have to put on the Horizon bookstore golf shirt and apron and come in and work."

Even as Dubas was shifting his beliefs on this front, he got pressure from the outside when he took over in Toronto. He heard from players and their agents who wanted Dubas to loosen the reins on the rules that help define a Lou Lamoriello organization. The things Lamoriello puts into place to create unity within the organization weren't particularly popular. It even came up in negotiations with John Tavares when he was picking a place to sign as the most sought-after unrestricted free agent in hockey.

Are you keeping the old rules?

"The dress code, the grooming, the shaving, the hair—they wanted to be able to express themselves a little bit," Dubas said. "They didn't feel like they could be themselves."

In the end, under his leadership, Dubas decided that there

would be dress code rules, but that grooming around hair and shaving was a personal choice. With that decision, the Maple Leafs lost a small portion of their identity under Lamoriello. Which is fine, if there's something else that makes a player feel part of a bigger experience with the organization. If not a morning shave, what made a player feel like they're part of the group in playing for the Maple Leafs?

"Speaking very bluntly, I think that's one of the issues that we have is that we don't have yet a definitive thing about us," Dubas answered. "Part of the issue of that is those things get developed when you have success."

At this point, this was a group still searching for it.

———————————————

On May 31, 2021, at a mostly empty Scotiabank Arena with seats hidden by stretched-out coverings featuring large corporate logos because of COVID restrictions, the Montreal Canadiens beat the Maple Leafs for the third consecutive playoff game to eliminate a stunned Leafs team. It was their sixth consecutive playoff series loss. It was their eighth consecutive loss with a chance to close out a series. After the final buzzer echoed, Canadiens goalie Carey Price was immediately surrounded by teammates hugging him and celebrating their unlikely win. Auston Matthews worked his way through the handshake line, respectfully patting a few Canadiens on their shoulders while shaking hands, but his look was completely vacant. It was a stunning loss. Bad enough that head coach Sheldon Keefe didn't address the team afterward.

When I first pitched this extended conversation with Dubas, he agreed in part because he was willing to talk about his learning process. Specifically, learning from failure. This playoff series now provided plenty of opportunity.

"This is the business we've chosen," Dubas said. "So knowing that you're going to fail and you're going to have moments like you're up three to one in a series against Montreal and they're going to come back and beat you and you're going to lose and it sucks and it's brutal. I think you learn so much, way more than . . ."

He paused.

"Well, we haven't ever won. We won in the American League, but this is a whole other level, right? I think you learn so much from the moments when you fail, the things you really believe in don't work or haven't worked yet. Are you able to still believe in them? Do you want to change them? How much is changing the whole system at large?"

These were the questions Dubas set out to answer in the short window of time after that handshake line and when we'd chat over coffee sitting at a small table in the fine arts section of a small-town bookstore. He let out a long exhale when I asked him what came next after another playoff disappointment. His wife, Shannon, had a baby in the middle of the series, so there was a dose of reality and perspective waiting for him at home. That it was a colicky baby left even less time for self-pity.

In his mind, the coming player exit interviews would be the most important of his tenure with the Maple Leafs. In the past, he did exit interviews together with Keefe, but this time they separated. He interviewed players at Scotiabank Arena's Platinum Club, while Keefe held his own meetings in his office. These Maple Leafs were loaded with veterans who had a ton of perspective— Jason Spezza, Zach Bogosian, Nick Foligno, Joe Thornton. Foligno was the big trade deadline addition that year, and in the moment he was acquired it was widely celebrated as the perfect addition. He could play in the middle or on the wing. He was captain material. He played with an edge. He was one of the reasons the Columbus Blue Jackets were able to beat the Maple Leafs in the 2020 qualifying round. But a back injury and nerve pain that shot down his right leg meant he wasn't the player he needed to be against the Canadiens.

"When I got there, it was a team that knew they had something special. There was a good bond on the group. It was about understanding we have this great bond, but how do we push through?" Foligno said. "It was a struggle for some of our big boys when we went up three to one and they couldn't deliver. That's where the bond is created. That's great, we all love each other, but how do we get over the hump? . . . Sometimes, you have to punch through the ceiling as hard as you can."

When Foligno sat down to talk to Dubas following that playoff series, that's what he was thinking.

This team will figure it out.

"You have a really unique thing. Don't overanalyze it," Foligno told Dubas. "It takes a while for teams to break through. There are a lot of teams that had to stay with their core before they broke through. You make a rash decision, that can be the unraveling of a lot more. There's a reason the core four works. You're not finding those players."

Foligno saw it happen firsthand with another group. He relayed a story to Dubas about the evolution he saw from the Tampa Bay Lightning. In 2019, the Columbus Blue Jackets earned their first franchise playoff series win by sweeping Tampa Bay. The loss stunned the Lightning, who were the Presidents' Trophy winners. In that playoff series, the Blue Jackets felt like they could get under the skin of the Lightning's best players. And they did. Lightning star Nikita Kucherov was suspended for Game 3 after boarding Blue Jackets defenseman Markus Nutivaara late in the third period of a blowout Blue Jackets win.

The Blue Jackets knew they could yap, they could hit the Lightning. They could negate skill with distraction. Dubas relayed what Foligno told him about the following season.

"The next year when we got in and played against them, we were going to do the same thing. 'Here we go again, we know how to beat these guys,'" Foligno said. "The difference . . . was they had had their moment where they had blown something and now you could tell, none of the stuff that worked the year before, they didn't give a shit about it. They didn't care about it. They had one goal and that was they had this long history of disappointments and they were done with it. They knew it was their opportunity and their time and none of that stuff was going to work."

Foligno expanded on those thoughts and how they tied to the Maple Leafs when we chatted by phone a couple of years later.

"You need those guys to show, 'I can play this way, have this attitude—*this is mine*. You're not going to faze me,'" Foligno said. "There is a recipe for success. In the playoffs, you have to have sand in there. You have to take your licks and sometimes you have to give it back. Tampa figured it out. That's what I was trying to say to Kyle. You couldn't faze [the Lightning]. They just kept coming and coming. In the bubble, it was a whole different team. And then, they got confidence off that. Now, when they used to break, you see it's not breaking. Now you feel invincible. That's how you win. You get that belief going, and boom."

From afar, Foligno saw it starting to take shape for the Maple

Leafs when they finally broke through the first round and beat the Lightning in six games during the 2023 playoffs.

"I remember [Auston] Matthews laughing when he would get grabbed," Foligno said. "As much as I understand what he's doing, sometimes if you grab back and stare the guy in the face, it's 'Oh, never mind.' You saw that he fought [Steven] Stamkos this year. It wasn't much of a fight, but at least he stood in there. In previous years, he didn't do that. Sometimes, they have to understand how bad they want it."

Dubas listened to everything Foligno relayed about his experience and filed it away.

He also met with Auston Matthews and saw a side of Matthews that rarely surfaces. Matthews, for all his superstardom, his fashion, his ability to score goals in a way unlike anyone of his generation, can be reserved. In his exit interview following the Canadiens loss, Matthews wasn't reserved. He wasn't quiet. In pleading with Dubas not to make massive changes to the core because of a disappointing series finish against the Canadiens, Matthews was passionate.

"He was the most animated and definitive I've ever heard him about anything, the group, and where it's at," Dubas said. "He was like, 'This group is going to get it done. We can't come apart because we just had three bad games.'"

The two dug in on that topic because this was at the heart of figuring out the next steps for the Maple Leafs. Was it really just three bad games? Or was there a deeper issue to root out? Dubas wasn't sure.

"To me, it's more than that," he said.

Dubas ran through the games that concerned him, over the leadership of two different general managers and two different coaching staffs. There was Game 7 against Montreal. Game 5 against Columbus. Games 6 and 7 against Boston the year before. Game 7 the year before that.

"I feel the team plays not to lose. It's like watching a championship boxing match where the two boxers go out. Rather than trying to assert your style or assert your gameplay, you get on your heels," Dubas explained.

Dubas listened to the opinion of his young superstar, but he wanted more.

———————

One of the small silver linings of having such a public, excruciating playoff loss is the response that comes from other people in leadership. They want to help.

After that Montreal loss, Dubas received calls from people offering advice and he also reached out to those who had suffered similar heartbreaks. The Washington Capitals were the most recent example of a team that battled through criticism and frustration to eventually win a Stanley Cup. There was a moment in time when it was publicly questioned whether a team could win with Alex Ovechkin, the greatest pure goalscorer to ever play the game, as the captain. There was a time when the perception was that Nicklas Backstrom was too soft. The team was light on grit. There were too many Europeans. Barry Trotz wasn't a playoff coach. Pick your criticism.

Capitals general manager Brian MacLellan isn't a big talker, but he's as forthcoming as they come when he does. He's a reader of stoic philosophy for fun. You're going to get a straight answer when you call him, which Dubas did after the loss to the Canadiens.

"It was great," Dubas said of the conversation. "You can say Washington is a different market than Toronto, but by that time, they had crossed that threshold. I remember, I lived it. I heard from other people in the game—they weren't going to win with these players . . . and so he said that everyone wanted massive changes and that's what was needed to appease everybody."

What massive changes did MacLellan implement in response?

"He did nothing," Dubas said. "Nothing. He did nothing at all."

I'd later relay this whole exchange to Dallas Stars GM Jim Nill and his face lit up in recognition. Toronto was just the latest NHL team to go through this. Before them, it was Washington. Nill has been around the game long enough to remember a time in which people wondered if Steve Yzerman could win.

"Washington? They were Detroit," Nill said. "Remember all those years Detroit couldn't make it? Went to the Final, lost to New Jersey. We went through the same thing. Blow it up. Can Yzerman lead?"

Nill was rolling.

"In Detroit, we couldn't win, man," he said. "Now you're sitting there and [team owners] the Ilitches are saying, 'What are you guys going to do? Blow it up? Can you win with Yzerman? Can you win with Fedorov? Can you do this?' In the end, we all got together and said, 'We're getting a hundred and ten points every year. Something is going right. We've just got to keep—give yourself a chance every year."

The story of Yzerman's evolution from an offensive-first superstar to a two-way center who ended up winning Stanley Cups on one leg is well told. Nobody is questioning his leadership credentials any longer. And in this moment in time, Dubas started seeing an evolution in his own captain, John Tavares. There was a transformation point in that season, when it was clear to Tavares for the first time in his life that he was no longer the top offensive player on the team.

"He was probably the third option, which is a difficult transition, which he told me in his exit meeting," Dubas said. "He said, 'This is the first time in my entire life that if we needed a goal, we needed something, it wasn't going to be my line or I was going to be the third or fourth guy.' Though we talked about it the previous summer at length, he realized it during the year. When he realized it and accepted it and embraced it, then he started to take off and play. And play well. Then unfortunately, we lost him."

Midway through the first period of Game 1 against the Montreal Canadiens, Ben Chiarot hit Tavares, who then immediately took a knee to the head from a trailing Corey Perry. Dubas was in his suite, standing next to assistant GM Brandon Pridham, banging on the counter in front of him in what looked like a plea to get help out to Tavares quickly. Tavares was stretchered off the ice, his series was over. And while it's fair to wonder how things might have ended differently if this collision never happened, the loss created opportunity for growth.

After the season, Tavares sent Dubas an article in which NBA coach Steve Kerr talked about his time playing on great teams with the Chicago Bulls and San Antonio Spurs. Kerr said that on both of those teams, if you were a bench player or the last player on the roster, your contribution was always noticed. It might be something done in a practice or in just a few minutes of playing time, but Kerr said those teams celebrated everybody's contributions. It made them feel like crucial players on those teams. Tavares sent it to Dubas with his opinion attached: "I think we do a pretty good job of this."

Dubas disagreed.

"I said to John, 'We don't. At all. Just take a look around you. When I look at it, I see a number of players on the team and they don't know how they really fit in.' Last year was an easy way for me to see this. Every single thing we did was together as a group. Especially in Canada. Every meal was in the ballroom of the hotel. Sheldon and I and whomever else. . . . You could see the same group of guys together at the same time. It was mostly the core players. You would see Ilya Mikheyev, Pierre Engvall, Travis Dermott—they were sort of on the outside. I said to John, 'We don't do a good job. In my opinion, you guys don't do a good job of that at all.'"

The players pushed back. Wasn't it the role of management and coaches to outline clearly to every player what their role is?

"We're not talking about role," Dubas said. "If a player in a very small role does something great, it's going to mean way more for him to hear from Auston, Mitch, John, Jason Spezza than . . . from the people who have an incentive for him to execute that role. His peers. . . . So John, to his credit, has taken on this focus."

At one point, Tavares was having a summer event at his cottage and he called Dubas to go over every player in the roster to talk about an invite and making them feel included. He was being intentional on how he changed as a captain.

"He's not a natural rah-rah guy. He's the best lead-by-example guy you could have," Dubas said. "Everything he does is at such a high level, but the key for him is trying, to me anyways, to bring others into that domain."

This was clearly an evolution. One forged by failure, by learning from mistakes. And as the conversation continued,

Dubas shared that Tavares was at the center of what he called his biggest mistake to that point of his tenure with the Maple Leafs.

———————

Walk past the windows covered by the distinctive striped awnings, under the American and Canadian flags, and into the marble-floored lobby of the Beverly Wilshire and there is someone waiting immediately to serve you. Maybe help with your bags after shopping at the nearby Louis Vuitton or Fendi store on Rodeo Drive.

But in the summer of 2018, on the weekend before the Maple Leafs shocked the hockey world by signing the biggest free agent in decades—John Tavares—Dubas needed a completely different kind of help. The night before, he'd sent a text to Tavares in the first moment he could communicate with him without breaking any league rules. The message was straightforward.

We think you'll be a great fit in Toronto.

There was no enjoying the luxury of the Beverly Hills hotel. Dubas was putting together a package to present to the Tavares camp and needed to figure out how to print it all out. At one point while getting ready to join Brendan Shanahan and Mike Babcock in making his pitch to Tavares at the nearby CAA offices, Dubas spotted Lou Lamoriello and Barry Trotz. In a matter of weeks, Lamoriello had gone from Leafs GM to Leafs special advisor to now the guy running the Islanders and competing for one of the best players in the league.

"This is the captain of [Lamoriello's] team. It was a moment of pure, kind of, guilt," Dubas said. "This is the guy who has given me so much. He's taken this job and now I'm trying to take from him something that is so . . ."

Dubas paused a moment and changed directions. "They're there, trying to put everything on the table to keep John."

It wasn't just these two organizations. Steve Yzerman, Julien BriseBois, and Jon Cooper were there trying to lure Tavares to Tampa Bay. During their meeting, Cooper watched Tavares with an intensity that suggested he was analyzing every reaction from Tavares as Yzerman or BriseBois spoke. San Jose made a massive pitch, with German billionaire owner Hasso Plattner driving two hours from Laguna to see Tavares in person. In a week of memorable moments, a cartoon featuring then–Sharks GM Doug Wilson's dog addressing Tavares's dog got laughs. Boston captain Patrice Bergeron got on the phone while the Bruins made their pitch.

But nobody outdid the Leafs.

Shanahan, Babcock, Dubas, John, and his wife, Aryne, joined agents Pat Brisson and Jim Nice in making their way to CAA's theater to watch a hype video the Leafs put together as part of their attempts to lure Tavares. As they approached the theater, actor Jason Bateman emerged.

"Shanny was like, 'Jason?' 'Shanny?' I was like, 'How do you guys know each other?'" Nice said. "I guess they used to pal around."

After the surprise reunion they settled in to watch a video that included the stitching of Tavares's name on a Maple Leafs jersey. In the video, the name and number found its way into the rafters.

"It was perfectly done," Nice said. "I think we all had the chills afterwards."

After the pitches, Tavares and Aryne joined Brisson and Nice in Pat's CAA office. All the coaches, GMs, and movie stars were gone. Tavares started sharing his thoughts. The San Jose pitch was really interesting. Staying in New York was still a very compelling draw. There was a belief that New York could probably offer more money than Toronto and San Jose—more than any of them. Before a decision was made, Dubas was contacted to answer follow-up questions. He'd spent time in Los Angeles, walking around the city, meeting with agents, and basically waiting out the clock until a decision was made on the Tavares front. Dubas suspected that the allure to win a Stanley Cup immediately in Tampa Bay, with Steven Stamkos and Victor Hedman, might really appeal to Tavares, even if the money wasn't as high as elsewhere. But if he had to make a bet, he really thought that Tavares would return to New York in the end. That is, until he got called back to talk to John and Aryne.

For the first meetings, there were media stakeouts and television camera guys in the streets outside the CAA building. When Dubas returned, there was none of that. This time, it was a clandestine operation.

"We had Kyle show up with a baseball cap and sunglasses on," Nice said.

They snuck him in the back of the building. It was Dubas alone with John and Aryne. No Bateman or hype film. No talk about the power play or wingers. It was questions from Aryne about how life would be in Toronto. The pressures of returning home. How the family would have to adapt. It wasn't about the player any longer. It was about the couple, their fit, and the rest of their lives together. There was also a question from Tavares about the core.

"If I come to Toronto, is it a one-year thing with this group or are you going to be able to keep the group together?" Tavares asked.

We're keeping the team together, Dubas answered. We're not doing all this for a one-year window. Plus, Dubas wasn't convinced the team was there yet to push all in for one year.

"These guys are still twenty-one years old, John," Dubas said. "Adding one player doesn't necessarily propel it. But it would make us more formidable."

When the meeting was over, that was the first moment Dubas believed the Maple Leafs had a real chance. On June 30, Brisson called to float the idea of Dubas discussing sign-and-trade options with the Islanders to get an eighth year on the books. It was getting serious. It was agreed that if Tavares wasn't going back to the Islanders, Lou Lamoriello shouldn't hear it from Dubas, and so Dubas waited to hear from his old boss. That evening, Dubas's phone rang and it was Lamoriello on the other end of the line. There was talk of a trade so that the Islanders could get a return for losing their captain, but it didn't get done. In the end, the lure to return home to try and win a Stanley Cup with the Maple Leafs led to Tavares and the Maple Leafs agreeing to a seven-year deal worth $77 million. It's a deal Dubas said he'd do in a heartbeat again. It also changed everything when it came to contract talks with the rest of the young stars in Toronto.

In Dubas's mind, there was a mistake made here, but it wasn't signing Tavares.

"The biggest mistake I think I've made in my whole time here has been not taking care of the three incumbent contracts. [William] Nylander was up. [Mitch] Marner and Matthews could have been done on July 1 extensions," Dubas said.

He heard the criticism about the amount paid to the three

young forwards. Or that they didn't get the right term. But to him, the mistake was in the timing. He believes he should have made more progress on those deals before focusing on the Tavares contract. Before the Maple Leafs signed Tavares, Dubas said he talked to all three players to let them know that this was something they were going to pursue.

"And if we went down this path, would they be on board with it potentially impacting them?" Dubas said, relaying the topic of those conversations. "But the thing I learned was that once we signed John to the [average annual value] we did, it lifted the lid on the entire ceiling."

The next big negotiation for Dubas was the William Nylander contract, and it didn't go particularly well. An opposing team let it be known they would sign Nylander to a deal worth $7 million per season, but needed the Maple Leafs to take money back in order to make it happen. That didn't help the cause.

"It's like, 'Okay, offer sheet him for that amount.' 'No, we need you to take this player.' Then the player gets that number in mind," Dubas said.

Dubas flew to New York to meet personally with Nylander's agent, Lewis Gross, to get it done. He flew to Switzerland to meet with Nylander one-on-one to get it done. It went down to the 5 p.m. deadline on a Saturday in December 2018 that, had the two sides missed it, Nylander would have had to sit out the season. With forty minutes before the deadline, Nylander said he called Dubas to get the deal done. And even in those final moments, his agent was reminding him what was at stake.

"The clock was a big part of that day. I remember saying to Willie, 'Willie, if we get this done, if we get this contract, you've got to get it right back,'" Gross said. "'We don't have a lot of time here. This isn't time to be too cool for school. Sign it right away.'"

They got it done. But it wasn't easy and it affected Nylander's season. Gross doesn't necessarily agree with Dubas's belief that the Tavares deal impacted Nylander or how the negotiation ended up proceeding. He suggested that every deal exists on its own. But Dubas can't help thinking it all could have played out differently.

"If we don't have John and we don't have that lid blown off, it's probably easy. In the end, William is the type of person who does every single thing at the last possible moment. I don't know, even going back to that, if it would have been any different," Dubas said. "The outcome is the outcome. I think his contract is actually a very good contract. Especially with the way he's performed."

I shared this story with Darryl Belfry, who was a player development coach for the Maple Leafs. We talked about the perception of those contracts being a mistake, and you could hear him getting worked up on the other end of the line.

"Take COVID out and I think about this all the time. What would the cap be? Ninety million dollars? They sign the contracts, the cap stays flat," Belfry said. "Kyle would never say it, but I will. I think that's part of it. . . . You have a world shut down, it knocks the cap to a flat cap for multiple years and you're stuck holding the bag on a projection. You didn't miscalculate. It's an act of nature that beats you."

Dubas's conclusion is to learn from it all. He does it by logging everything. Every conversation he has, every decision he makes. He does it so he can go back and assess the thinking, assess the process. He takes detailed notes in a Moleskine journal. When it rises to the level of a conversation with another GM or agent, he puts it into a Google doc that tags players being discussed for easy reference later. Every conversation is time-stamped and tracked.

"You think you're going to remember everything, but you don't," Dubas said.

It helps the decision-making process. It helps the learning. He has no problem looking back at this moment in time and coming to two conclusions. Signing John Tavares was a good idea. Focusing only on signing John Tavares wasn't.

"That to me was an experience issue," he said. "I had to go through that and have it have an impact on our team that I don't think many would say is positive—prolonged contract discussions with two of our best players, one of them missing two months of the season and then having a bad year because of it. All those different things that could have set our team up better, I've learned from mistakes. Looking back on it, they're my mistakes. I know that because I've logged everything."

It's all part of learning on the job, an intentional process to get better. He did that in Toronto, the payoff will have to come in Pittsburgh. As we were getting ready to leave Horizon Books, I offered to buy him something to read. I felt like it was the least I could do. We'd been talking for hours.

"You don't have to buy me a book," he answered.

I suggested we should do it for the bookstore. Small town. Help a small business.

"I'll buy a book for the bookstore," he said.

We walked toward the checkout when we passed the travel section. There was a book by Anthony Bourdain that caught his eye called *World Travel*. He picked it up and said it reminded him of a quote he just saw from Bourdain on Instagram.

He found the quote and started reading it.

Eat at a local restaurant tonight.
Get the cream sauce.
Have a cold pint at 4 o'clock in a mostly empty bar.
Go somewhere you've never been...

He placed the book on the counter in front of the woman at checkout. She looked at it, then scanned it.

"All set?" she asked.

"All set."

CHAPTER 4

TRUSTING YOUR INSTINCTS

Do what you think needs to be done and not what the perception is.

—**Brian MacLellan**

Brian MacLellan was walking through the lobby of the Eau Palm Beach Resort. Lumbering, really. He's a big fella. A Stanley Cup–winning NHL forward turned lawyer turned Stanley Cup–winning general manager, he's six foot three with catcher's-mitt hands. He worked his way up to the NHL through college hockey, not a typical path for a kid born in Guelph, Ontario. He developed under legendary college coach Ron Mason, scoring thirty-four goals as a freshman at Bowling Green. It was a total that would have led the team if his close friend George McPhee hadn't put up forty.

The Capitals general manager since 2014 is reserved but has a sneaky good sense of humor. When we exchanged texts the previous day to talk, it was the first conversation between us in nearly three years. He shot back: "Where have you been hiding?"

I explained. Asked to meet up. And here he was, walking through the lobby of this five-star Florida resort, underneath its crystal chandeliers and toward a terrace overlooking the Atlantic Ocean. Giant blue patio umbrellas provided shade to those stretching out on the blue-and-white-striped lounge chairs. The other guests around us were in bathing suits, enjoying the mix of waves crashing with the music being played by the pool. There was a hint of sunscreen in the air, plus the scent of what anyone walking by was drinking. We might have been the only ones in the area in slacks and polo shirts not on the hotel payroll.

I caught a break when MacLellan decided not to join his fellow GMs on the traditional Monday afternoon golf trip following the first full day of March's annual GM meetings. Instead, he was using the afternoon to recover from what had been a draining stretch on the job. I asked how he was holding up.

"Frustrated with our year, a lot of injuries, a lot of stuff," he said, settling in with his back facing the pool and the ocean. "It's been constant."

A few weeks earlier, Tarik El-Bashir wrote in *The Athletic* that MacLellan met with star Alex Ovechkin to loop him in on the Capitals trade deadline plans. Key players who helped Ovechkin break through in 2018 with his first Stanley Cup were most likely going to be traded, including Ovechkin's close friend Dmitry Orlov. MacLellan sent an email out to his fellow general managers to let them know the organization was open to moving its veterans and the sale was on. Orlov was the first to go. On February 23, the Capitals acquired three draft picks, including a first-rounder from the Bruins for the veteran defenseman. Five days later, Marcus Johansson was sent to the Minnesota Wild. That same day, MacLellan flipped the Bruins pick into young defenseman Rasmus Sandin in a trade with the Maple Leafs. Then the final move was a trade that sent Lars Eller to the Colorado Avalanche for another pick.

This was a series of transactions that ripped apart a former Cup winner.

It was Eller who dug a puck out from behind Marc-André Fleury and buried it home with 7:37 remaining in the third period of Game 5 of the 2018 Stanley Cup Final against the Vegas Golden Knights. The goal that sent a sea of red outside in Washington, D.C., into absolute bedlam. It ended up being the clincher. But when you talk to people inside the organization, that's not even the biggest goal he scored during that playoff run.

No game was more critical during the Capitals' run to the Stanley Cup than Game 3 of their opening-round series against the Columbus Blue Jackets. The Capitals dropped the first two games of that series at home. They probably should have lost the third game in Columbus. With the game tied at two and 1:16 remaining in regulation, Columbus star Artemi Panarin took a one-time feed from Zach Werenski and fired a shot off the left post, the ringing audible up in the press box. In overtime, Cam Atkinson banged one off the other post. These Blue Jackets seemed determined to bury the Capitals in a three-game deficit and put an end to it all, and probably change the future of the franchise dramatically. But with eleven minutes remaining in the second overtime, Brett Connolly fired a shot that Sergei Bobrovsky blocked, with the rebound bouncing to his left. Zach Werenski's clearing attempt was blocked by Lars Eller, and after a couple deflections somehow the puck found its way in. Just like that, the game was over. The Capitals were back in the series. If any of those Columbus shots had scored, the history of this franchise and those running it might be completely different. It's a perspective to keep in mind, just how much luck is part of the process when it comes to winning hockey championships.

"We talk about it all the time. All the time. Game 3 of the first round, we're about to go down three-oh to the Blue Jackets and who knows what happens after that if we get swept in the first round," said Zach Leonsis, son of owner Ted Leonsis and president of media and new enterprises with Monumental Sports. "Lars Eller comes back and scores the overtime winner and then we win every game after that [in the series] and we go on to win the Stanley Cup. It was inches away."

Inches. So yeah, trading Lars Eller hurt. Trading all of those players hurt.

"It wasn't easy," MacLellan said. "Plus, you get everyone to hate you, you know?"

This is the part of being a general manager people don't often see. The Capitals coaching staff was mad at MacLellan. They didn't care what the playoff percentage chances were at the time these deals were made, they were still trying to win games. Players were mad, too. Ovechkin's close friend was gone. The guy who scored a goal that changed a franchise and knit a group of players together for eternity was gone, too. These weren't just transactions, these were legacies leaving.

"You're ripping guys out of the room that you've won a Cup with," MacLellan said. "It rips the fucking heart out of the players, you know? They're like, 'What the fuck is going on?' They don't care about the future, retooling. 'Don't give me any of that fucking crap, it's my buddy you just got rid of.' . . . You're calling guys and they're saying goodbye to everybody at practice."

The pain was still very real at this point. While you're winning with these players, you also get to know their families. You know the young kids. MacLellan understands there's a barrier between the players and management, but even that barrier only reaches so high. Become too detached and your humanity is lost. MacLellan's humanity is very much in place. In that moment in the Florida resort, it was clear the job was wearing on him. Building a Stanley Cup winner is way more fun than tearing one down. Even if you want to call it a retool or something much less gut-wrenching. I shared my theory that it should probably be a different general manager ultimately in charge of going through the rebuild than the one who won a Stanley Cup. He didn't disagree.

"You need new energy, you know?" he said. "I'm at a certain age where I'm going to be winding down here, too. I think my skill set was good for the stage we were at over the last ten years. It's probably better for someone fresh to come in at some point here. We've got to get through the next three years, see how we can do, and then it's new [when] Ovi's gone, all these guys are gone. The transition has to happen then, to a new guy. I think."

It was not an easy moment in time for the guy who helped build the first Stanley Cup–winning team in Capitals history. But that was not why I wanted to chat.

One of the things so admirable about the hockey community is how willing those who have had success are to help those still finding their way. It manifests itself in different forms. Sometimes it's an NHL coach running a penalty kill seminar during the summer for a group of youth coaches. Or Gordie Howe sharing advice with a young Wayne Gretzky on what it means to be an ambassador of the sport. Or Cammi Granato showing up at a Nike camp to give advice on winning in the Olympics to a group of women who grew up idolizing her.

Maybe it happens in different sports, but it definitely does in hockey. So when Kyle Dubas called Brian MacLellan to talk to him about how to persevere through crushing playoff disappointment, there was never any hesitation to share all he'd learned. And if anyone knew playoff disappointment and the criticism that follows, like Dubas was experiencing as the Leafs GM in 2021 after getting eliminated by the Canadiens, it was MacLellan and his Capitals.

In 2017, the Capitals suffered a Game 7 loss to the Pittsburgh Penguins that led to one of the most crushing postgame scenes I'd ever witnessed. It was the third consecutive second-round exit for a team that should have been a powerhouse. The media walked from player to player, looking for answers, when it was clear there weren't any. T. J. Oshie, covered in sweat, searched for words.

"You almost wonder how much disappointment you have to put yourself through before you can find a way to get the job done," Oshie said that night.

In that moment, I honestly thought we were seeing the end of the Capitals as we knew them. I'd find out later, there were players on that roster who felt strongly that dramatic change was the best path forward. MacLellan was the man charged with fixing years of underachieving in the playoffs by a team loaded with talent, and Dubas reached out to know what went into the decisions that followed.

"I went through our experience," MacLellan said. "The narrative is the same and we had the same type of teams where we had skilled teams. Really good during the season."

And then?

"Underperforming."

If a championship ring and years of distance had buried the frustrations that came with those underachieving teams, some of the emotion started to resurface as MacLellan recalled that era of helping lead the Capitals. Three consecutive postseason appearances were ended by the New York Rangers. After that, the rival Pittsburgh Penguins ended things in consecutive seasons. A team loaded with talent couldn't get out of the second round.

"You get the same fucking opponent every fucking round. It's like, 'Pittsburgh again? Right away?'" MacLellan said. "You make the argument we were the two best teams in the league. But you still got to get through it, you know?"

Like Dubas did after losing to the Canadiens in 2021, MacLellan guided the Capitals through soul-searching exit interviews following that Game 7 loss to the Penguins in 2017. He asked questions to get feedback, but he offered players a chance to vent their frustration. To get their anger out and express what they felt needed to be done.

Veteran defenseman Brooks Orpik was the first to go.

"It went by age," Orpik said when we chatted about those conversations.

In May of 2014, the Washington Capitals promoted MacLellan from assistant GM under McPhee to become McPhee's replacement. One of his first big moves was signing Orpik to a five-year deal worth $27.5 million, and it was a contract not universally applauded. On the day it was signed, a writer for CBS Sports concluded: "At that price, this deal is already looking like a bad one for the Capitals." The logic from those critical was that Orpik wasn't a great skater and was also starting to show his age. A tough combination. But to MacLellan, this was a deal made to start changing the culture of a team that needed to learn how to win. When he arrived, Orpik was very aware that the last thing teammates wanted was for him to come in and tell everyone how things were done in Pittsburgh. He wasn't about to share a bunch of Sidney Crosby leadership stories. But the Capitals players were curious. What made it work in Pittsburgh? How was Crosby as a leader?

The one area Orpik highlighted was practice habits.

"Sid is a guy who doesn't say a ton, but he is the hardest-working guy every single day in practice," he said. "With his stature, it forces everybody else to follow."

Working closely with coach Barry Trotz, Orpik tried to pick his spots in sharing some of that feedback and helping push the work ethic beyond what the Capitals were doing in the past. There was one point when the team got off to a slow start during the season that the two realized there was work to be done on this front.

"I remember saying, 'Hey, there's just so many things that have been done a certain way for so long, it's going to be tough to weed out some of these bad habits and cultural issues here that might be plaguing some of the success,'" Orpik said.

By the time the 2017 playoffs arrived, those issues had been ironed out. The players felt like this team was in its best position to win, and that's what made that Penguins loss so hard. For the player exit interviews, there were ten minutes slotted for each of the players to meet with MacLellan. When Orpik finished his conversation, he walked into the hallway, and there were at least five or six players in line waiting.

His conversation had lasted over an hour.

"Mac was really digging and probing," Orpik said. "I really want to win. I want to help Mac out because I want to win. But you're also not throwing anyone under the bus here. You're kind of caught. It's a tough wire you're walking on there."

"It was exhausting," MacLellan said.

When I pressed Orpik for details of the conversations, he paused.

"How honest was Mac?"

MacLellan certainly comes off as honest. He's direct in his answers and he's often direct when he's not willing to give an answer. In this case, he did both. According to MacLellan, two very clear solutions from the players emerged from those exit interviews. If he was going to follow the advice from his team during those lengthy conversations, they had two strong recommendations.

What were the two things?

"I'm not telling you," MacLellan answered. "It affects people. It's just a private thing. I'd be breaking a big trust thing because everybody opened up, one hundred percent."

Not only wasn't he sharing what those two things were, you can't even go back and look at transactions or moves MacLellan made that summer for clues. Management heard the recommendations from the players. They didn't do any of it.

"We chose to fight through those issues the next season," MacLellan said, "which could have been a disaster."

Orpik wasn't giving it up, either.

"I know what the two things were, kind of the collective response, and they did neither," he said before offering a question that marveled at the decision to ignore the two recommendations.

"Looking back even more, gathering all that information, how did they not pull the trigger on one of those things?"

Dick Patrick helped explain. He's been with the organization since 1982. He's the chairman of the entire organization. His grandfather was Lester Patrick, who won two Stanley Cups as a player with the Montreal Wanderers in 1905 and 1906 before going on to coach and manage the New York Rangers. His father, Muzz, won a Stanley Cup with the Rangers in 1940.

"Growing up as a boy, going with my dad to Rangers games, [I learned] the players are such good people, straightforward people. You can't be dishonest on the ice and be successful," Patrick said.

The most successful teams have that kind of honesty, he explained. There's also respect for each other, from the best player to the last guy on the roster to the team services person.

"A team doesn't win just because of one or two stars or the smartest coaching," he said. "It wins from having great effort and support and performance from everyone."

But to Patrick, there are limits to that honesty. Emotions cloud judgment. When you ask for an assessment coming off an emotionally draining series, the solution that emerges isn't always reasoned.

"First of all, players work so hard and put their everything into it every year. When you don't win, those exit interviews, they're not going to be happy. They're going to be very candid. Oftentimes it's 'This teammate has to go,'" Patrick said. "They work so hard at it. Everything is there to win. They never expect to lose when they're in a playoff series. When they do, they feel something went terribly wrong. What is it?"

In this case, they pointed in two directions. Neither taken by

Capitals management. And the following season, the Capitals finally broke through and won a Stanley Cup, escaping the first round by a matter of inches. That's how perilous each decision is when running an NHL team.

"So I told Kyle that," MacLellan said. "Trust your instincts, do what you think needs to be done and not what the perception is. And if it's this serious, like our issues—you assume he has [similar but] different things—I said, 'You make the choice and live with it.' . . . It's not what everybody else thinks. The players aren't always correct and the coaches aren't always correct and the fans definitely aren't always correct in their assessment. The media, the fans, the whole thing."

McLellan's conclusion?

"He has to make his decisions."

The trip to Florida didn't provide all the answers I was looking for. But it did open up new paths because it was clear there was a lot to learn from the Capitals and the battles they had to fight before winning a championship. Cycling through coaches. Moving on from George McPhee, who assembled the foundation of the Stanley Cup winners before being fired. Replacing him with his close friend.

There were fascinating choices made along the way in Washington, D.C., and the best place to get clarity was at the very top of the organization.

———————————————————

Ted Leonsis has owned the Capitals since 1999. He won the Stanley Cup in 2018. He owns the WNBA's Washington Mystics and won a championship with that franchise a year later. He owns the NBA's Washington Wizards, an NBA G League team, and has a controlling interest in the esports Team Liquid. But more than anything, he's a media guy. He's owned magazines, written a book, created a board game, was certainly the first NHL owner to have his own blog, and definitely the only one with a book featuring sportswriting from the *New Yorker* edited by David Remnick resting behind his desk. He was also an internet visionary, consistently showing an ability to glimpse around the corner to see what's coming next in media.

"He looks at the world in unique ways," his son, Zach, explained.

Zach told how his dad would frame things while he was president of AOL. Other people at the company saw AOL's biggest competition as Microsoft, home of Microsoft Network and MSN Messenger. Leonsis would correct them and say that their biggest competitor was *Seinfeld*. Zach shared how his dad would explain it to his employees: "'Most people are coming home from work at six or six thirty, they're having a quick bite to eat, they want to relax, they're watching TV, and *Seinfeld* is the highest-rated sitcom on television, that's how people are spending their time. We need to find a way to make the internet and AOL more entertaining for the three hours of leisure that people have after work.'"

Leonsis understands that he's competing for time. He competed for time when creating media, and he's doing it as owner of the Capitals. When he first bought the team, he reached out to all the season ticket holders to hear what needed to be done for them to spend their time and money on the Capitals. He called one response the best email he's ever received.

A fan wrote that he loves the Capitals, but he also loves beer. So he shows up to every game early, buys two giant cups of beer, and drinks them during the first period. Then, with three minutes remaining in the period, in order to beat the rush, he goes up to the concession stand to buy two more beers. Then he heads to the bathroom. At this point, the logistics get difficult because he can't balance the beers on the urinals, so it means setting them on the floor in the bathroom. Not a pleasant experience. Leonsis considered the feedback, tested it out himself, and discovered the guy was absolutely right. He assigned his staff to find a solution.

Leonsis works hard to please fans. He works hard to create a winning atmosphere. He also works equally hard to please his investors and those he's in business with, and at times, each of those goals conflict with one another. For as much success as Leonsis has had as the owner in Washington, D.C., it isn't always perfect.

When I entered his office to talk through all of this, I realized quickly I was catching him on a unique day. As he settled into a chair across from me at a table in his office, a television above him was tuned in to the business show *Power Lunch*. The big news of the day was the IPO of a fast-casual restaurant called Cava, and the stock was taking off.

Leonsis was smiling. Every time the Cava stock ticked higher on the screen behind him, he was worth more. It turns out, he was an early investor in this Greek food chain.

"It looks like the IPO market is back, created by Cava, a D.C.-based company," Leonsis said. "I'm really proud of these young people who created it and we backed them, but it's D.C., not New York. Not Silicon Valley. We're sometimes so humble and modest, but there's a case study that we reopened the IPO market for business. Right now."

There's no questioning Leonsis's business acumen. He was out front in media. He was out front in sports betting and esports.

He seemed to be out front in fast-casual Greek food. He understood the power of the internet well before most people. Even
his approach to sports ownership—capture as much of a market
as possible and then control the means in which the games are
distributed—seems destined to pay off. Still, all of this business
success doesn't always align with running and building a hockey
team. Leonsis has had to evolve over the years, and it might have
been MacLellan who provided the most clarity on that front.

Hockey has a team-first culture that makes it unique. It's impossible to succeed on the back of one or two players, so many of
the best teams have adopted a culture in which individualism is
secondary to the needs of the team. When it becomes bastardized,
this collective mentality can be toxic and lead to hockey's ugliest
off-ice moments, like the Chicago Blackhawks failing to act when
informed of sexual assault allegations against then–video coach
Brad Aldrich during the 2010 playoffs.

When it's healthy and everyone is pulling together in pursuit
of a Stanley Cup, it's powerful. Those organizations that can set
aside personal agendas to work toward a larger goal are the ones
that end up winning consistently. And those winning organizations often create a sacred space for the players where they can
focus solely on the task at hand—winning hockey games.

Sometimes, the things that made Leonsis a great businessman
impeded on that culture of winning hockey. His enthusiasm to
create a connection with the fans to a star like Alex Ovechkin
through social media or a blog post interfered with those trying
to create a team culture. Or moments when Leonsis's loyalty to
his business partners and willingness to provide access behind the
scenes interfered with creating a sacred space for the players.

"Ted, like most other owners, was very successful and wealthy for his other business interests," said Dick Patrick, who has been working with Leonsis since day one of his ownership. "They're used to, when something is not going right . . . taking drastic action, laying off ten thousand people, or whatever they do in those organizations. It's not that easy in hockey. You might want to hire more scouts or update the practice facility, but no, it just doesn't work that way."

There needs to be hierarchy. There need to be boundaries. MacLellan's raw honesty and assessment of where Leonsis needed to change helped land him the job as McPhee's replacement. After firing longtime GM George McPhee in 2014, the Capitals conducted an extensive search to replace him, and there was definitely a view from fans and those around the team that an outside perspective would benefit the Capitals. MacLellan did not start the process at the top of the list.

"Frankly, we interviewed Brian to be nice," Leonsis said. "I had never been in a meeting with Brian, I had never really heard his voice."

That would change. MacLellan went through the interview process with nothing to lose and took advantage. He expressed his opinion on how Leonsis should operate and, at the very least, thought he might be helping out the next person on the job. He talked about hierarchy and boundaries. How he felt communication should work. If Leonsis had an issue, he should notify Dick Patrick and Patrick should notify the general manager. MacLellan believed that the owner shouldn't bypass people in the process when he communicated. And the opposite was true. If he had an issue, he'd go to Patrick. There had to be a layer of organizational hierarchy.

"I can't go to Ted. Ted can't come to me and go, 'What the

fuck? Trade this guy, get rid of that guy.' We tried to establish that," MacLellan said.

MacLellan took full advantage of the knowledge he'd acquired over thirteen years with the organization, including the previous seven as McPhee's assistant general manager. He noticed the impact on the players when Leonsis would walk in the dressing room and go straight to Alex Ovechkin or Nicklas Backstrom, bypassing others along the way. He witnessed the impact when so many of Leonsis's blog posts were about Ovechkin instead of others on the team. In a hockey world where the goal is creating an environment where everybody is pulling together equally, it can send an unintended message when the owner appears focused only on the biggest stars. He also told Leonsis to stop tweeting about players.

"I said, 'Good for you. I can do that,'" Leonsis said.

"I think if you're a successful businessperson, you think you can apply those skills to everything. That's hard. That's dangerous," MacLellan said. "There's a culture in hockey that's there, so I think as an outsider, you've got to learn it. You've got to be aware of certain things, how people react, how they move through everything. The hockey people, it's different."

In hockey, often the hierarchy revolves around the players. Take the team bus, for instance. In Washington, the players exit first, starting with the most experienced players and then down to the rookies. After the players are off, management and coaches can exit. The Capitals players are the first to get their hotel keys on the road. They're small things, but if you want players to feel ownership of the team, you treat them like the owners. MacLellan had strong opinions on how things needed to change and was asking for the ability to do it.

"I said, 'If you're not happy with the job I'm doing at any

point, you should say, "Let's get a new guy," ' " MacLellan said. "It just makes sense. But let me do my job."

Leonsis listened and mentioned to Dick Patrick afterward just how different a message MacLellan delivered compared to other candidates.

"They all tell me I'm the greatest. 'You're the best owner. . . . Everything is great.' They wanted the job," Leonsis said. "It was really interesting that the outsiders were telling us what we wanted to hear and the insider took the risk to tell us, 'All is not that great obviously and here are the things to do,' and so he won the job. And he did exactly what he said he was going to do quickly."

MacLellan's honesty and pointed way of communicating landed him the job. It was his honesty and clarity in advising Dubas that led me to this office. All in the effort of trying to figure out how to persevere through the toughest challenges to accomplish something great.

"You've got a good thread," Leonsis said.

So I kept pulling.

When the Washington Capitals hired George McPhee in June 1997 with coach Ron Wilson, he was just thirty-eight years old, the youngest general manager in hockey. A year later, the Capitals were playing for a Stanley Cup in the Final against the powerhouse Detroit Red Wings. In a *Washington Post* story leading into the series, the late Jennifer Frey expertly captured McPhee and Wilson in that moment. Wilson was in the spotlight, the outspoken coach front and center of the surprising Capitals run. McPhee was in the shadows, crediting former GM David Poile with building a roster he was able to tweak to surprising success. Frey put it perfectly in summing up McPhee's approach: "He didn't rip apart the team and remake it in his own image, just because he had that power. He didn't make big, sweeping moves to announce his presence. He sat back and decided to figure out what had gone wrong first, and how to fix the problem second. It was the best thing he could have done."

"What I had to do was move the furniture around," McPhee told Frey.

It was the moves that followed this surprising run that set up years of success and eventually a Stanley Cup. A couple of years before the 2004–05 lockout, Dick Patrick suggested that the team should start removing salary in order to have flexibility under the new salary cap he anticipated coming in the future. At first, McPhee held off.

"Then the next year we get through the year and Dick brought it up again and this time Ted said, 'Yeah.' And I said, 'Yeah,'" McPhee said. "We were all in agreement, let's tear it down."

In January of 2004, the Capitals sent Jaromir Jagr to the Rangers for Anson Carter. They traded Peter Bondra for Brooks Laich and a pick. As the trade deadline closed in, they shipped Robert Lang to the Red Wings for Tomas Fleischmann and a first-round pick that became Mike Green. They traded Sergei Gonchar to the Bruins for Shaone Morrisonn and a first-rounder that became defenseman Jeff Schultz.

The teardown was on. At one point in the process, with the deadline closing in, McPhee got a call from Colorado Avalanche GM Pierre Lacroix, who was interested in goalie Olaf Kolzig, and he made it clear the interest was strong.

Tell me what you need to get this done.

Kolzig was a fan favorite and moving him was a step in the teardown that McPhee said Leonsis wasn't willing to make. The Capitals' reluctance only drove the the potential offer even more. One first-round pick became two. The package could have been a big one.

"I remember that specifically," Patrick said. "By the time we got to Olie, it was like we were getting a little battle-fatigued. So many of the fan favorites are going out. There's no fan favorites coming back. Instead, it's a draft pick. Looking back when George was talking about Olie, probably both Ted and I got a little shell-shocked by then."

In this case, Leonsis's refusal to deal a popular player was probably shortsighted. I'd find out during our conversation that another time it happened, the ending was much different. The Capitals' teardown resulted in only three years of missing the playoffs, aided in large part by a stroke of lottery luck that landed them Alex Ovechkin. Drafting players like Backstrom, Green, Semyon Varlamov, Braden Holtby, John Carlson, and Dmitry Orlov in the coming years helped, too.

This group won a lot of games. It played an entertaining brand of hockey. But under McPhee, they never broke through in the playoffs. On April 3, 2013, the Capitals traded prospect Filip Forsberg to the Nashville Predators for Martin Erat. The Capitals had the foresight to pick Forsberg eleventh overall in 2012 in a draft that also landed them Tom Wilson, Chandler Stephenson, Connor Carrick, and Christian Djoos. But after getting a closer look at Forsberg following that draft, organizational doubts crept in. Coaches didn't love his game at the summer prospect camp. Viewings of him playing in Sweden led to reports back to

McPhee that included concerns about the lack of start and stop in his game. There wasn't enough compete.

The criticism was premature. Forsberg blossomed into a star after the trade.

"That's why both George and [coach Adam Oates] lost their jobs," Leonsis said. "Literally, what happened there was, the last minute, there's this huge trade, Martin Erat for Forsberg, and we thought Adam said, 'We're going to the playoffs, we need a money guy, experienced guy,' and what we heard afterwards was George makes the trade, Erat shows up, and Adam says, 'I don't want this guy.'"

After getting fired by the Capitals on April 26, 2014, McPhee landed in Vegas, where he put on a master class on how to build an expansion team, winning a Stanley Cup just six years into the existence of the franchise. Leonsis had just exchanged messages with McPhee when we chatted and any hard feelings that came with the departure were mended by the championships each of these franchises won in the years after the firing.

The Stanley Cup is a powerful thing.

"I spoke with George McPhee today. George worked for us for seventeen years and we made a move . . . and then he got hired to launch Vegas and has done *the* best job ever on a start-up in pro sports," Leonsis said. "Had we not won a Stanley Cup, I'm not sure I would feel the same way. But all of a sudden, we can honestly be magnanimous in the sharing of the joy. . . . When you hold the Cup, you can't describe it. That was my email to George, 'It's indescribable, isn't it?'"

Later, when I'd chat with McPhee about the emotions of winning the Stanley Cup, he described it in terms I had never heard before.

It brought out feelings he never anticipated.

Leonsis had a similar experience. In his case, the overflow of emotions came in the form of tears from one of the best players to ever play for the Capitals.

On June 7, 2018, the Washington Capitals were in Las Vegas playing the Golden Knights with a 3–1 series lead in the Stanley Cup Final. As the third period closed in on its halfway point, the Golden Knights held a one-goal lead. The talk among the Capitals on the bench was that they didn't want to let the Golden Knights back into the series. The players also were well aware that their families had been chartered into town. If they were able to win, there was a memorable night to be had in one of the best party towns in the world.

"There might have been some joking around, 'This would be pretty damn cool to celebrate in Vegas,'" Brooks Orpik said.

With 10:11 remaining in the game, it was Orpik who kept the puck in at the blue line, firing a shot toward his former teammate Marc-André Fleury. Capitals forward Devante Smith-Pelly redirected the shot with his skate as he was sprawling through the air, beating Fleury with a shot. The game was tied. A few minutes later, the combination that sank the Blue Jackets in double OT during a must-win first-round game—a Brett Connolly shot followed by a Lars Eller rebound—gave the Capitals the lead. It would end up being the Stanley Cup winner, the shot that gave the Caps their first championship in their forty-four-year history. From the moment NHL commissioner Gary Bettman handed the Stanley Cup to Alex Ovechkin, the celebration was on.

Since the game was an early start, the players got an extended celebration at the arena with friends and family. Then the party moved to the Mandarin Oriental, where there was a reception on the third floor with family, players, and everyone else in the organization. As the night went on, the party extended to the MGM, where buses dropped the team off and Ovechkin, in a pink button-down and the Stanley Cup in his hand, led a group through the lobby toward Hakkasan, a Vegas nightclub. In a TMZ clip for the ages, Ovechkin is holding the Cup high as lasers shoot in time to pulsating music, falling confetti surrounding him and DJ Tiësto by his side.

But it was the ballroom celebration at the team hotel that led to an exchange Leonsis won't forget. He walked in and the players were already celebrating hard, as they would for weeks. He spotted Nicklas Backstrom with the Cup, having a great time. Backstrom looked over at Leonsis, spotted him and his wife, Lynn, and ran over with the Cup. He handed it to Leonsis.

"And he starts crying," Leonsis said. "And he goes, 'Thank you, I love you, thank you. I'm an idiot.'"

Leonsis laughed retelling what Backstrom said to him.

"'I can't believe I said, "I [don't] think we're going to win a Stanley Cup. Thank you for not listening to me,"'" Leonsis said in sharing Backstrom's response at the celebration. "It was a very endearing moment."

Thank you for not listening to me.

A moment for the ages was created by Leonsis's refusal to give in to Backstrom's trade request following that crushing loss to the Penguins in the 2017 playoffs. After the elimination game, a large group of players had dinner together at the steakhouse at the MGM National Harbor in Maryland. Team Sweden management was pushing hard to get Backstrom out of the United States to Cologne, Germany, to join the team in the World Championships.

"Team Sweden was all over him and he said, 'I'm going to dinner with these guys. If you guys want me you can wait another day,'" Orpik said. "Knowing Nicky, that's not surprising."

There was a lot of discouragement at that dinner. A lot of frustration. Everyone felt like it was a blown opportunity, with maybe the best roster ever assembled in Washington. The pressure from the outside was mounting, as was the criticism. The exit interviews were emotional and lengthy. It was under these circumstances that Backstrom openly questioned whether he and Ovechkin could win together in Washington.

"He came to us after the season and said, 'It's not working,'" Leonsis said. "'It's obvious something is wrong in this mix. And so I think it's time for you to consider whether Alex and I make a good team and will we ever be able to win a Stanley Cup? I'm at that point in my career where, if I don't win a Stanley Cup, I'll be unfulfilled. Can it happen here? For the first time, I'm really questioning that. So much so that I want you to consider—should I be traded?'"

I asked Leonsis if it was a demand.

"Well . . . ," he said, and laughed. "None of our bedrock players, they never threw a hand grenade in and said this is going to blow up."

Backstrom went to the World Championships, put up seven points in five games playing on a line with MVP William Nylander, and scored in the shootout of the gold medal game to beat Canada. But the success there didn't change his frustrations with the Capitals. Leonsis said he returned to the United States and continued meeting with management.

"He was filled with angst and uncertainty, and it was so dramatic that Mac said, 'Ted, you need to come in and hear him out and be involved,'" Leonsis said. "Nick came and laid out what his concerns were and the data that he saw. And why he felt angst and was shaken in his belief and was pretty amped up about it. And I had been there when we signed Nick to the big contract extensions. I watched him as a rookie all the way through to this pivotal moment and I said, 'I hear you, I understand and I understand the emotion in it and I share in the angst. But I believe in our plan. I believe in our core. I believe in you. I believe in Alex and I'm not trading you. I'm not going to allow your request to go out into the market. No.'"

The payoff was a Stanley Cup, celebrated with a heartfelt apology from Backstrom. A championship won by the tiniest of margins—an inch here or there against Columbus in round one would have derailed the whole thing. Maybe those trade demands get louder the following summer.

Now those are all just what-ifs. The Capitals won their Stanley Cup. They got their celebration in Vegas, beating McPhee's Golden Knights. On my final trip for this book, I'd get a chance to sit down with McPhee to hear how he finally broke through with a championship. But first, a few weeks after meeting with Leonsis, was a visit to New Jersey to go behind the scenes with someone who not only helped lead a team to a gold medal as captain. She fundamentally changed the sport of hockey in the United States forever.

CHAPTER 5

TURNING DETAILS INTO GOLD

It wasn't easy at the time. I made a lot of enemies along the way, pushing people where they didn't want to be pushed, pushing myself where I didn't want to be pushed. The end goal was to win. To be perfect.

—Meghan Duggan

Meghan Duggan was sitting across the table from me. We were in a private room at the Prudential Center in Newark, New Jersey, and the Devils staff was just outside the door eating. There was constant movement in the hallways and dressing room around the corner as the organization's prospects were running through a tight schedule of events surrounding the annual summer camp.

This was Duggan's show.

She placed her phone down on the table in front of us and set an alarm for 1:27 p.m. That's as late, to the minute, as we could talk without her delaying a team bus she'd arranged to take the Devils prospects to a community event.

"We can find time tomorrow, too," she said, maybe noticing me eyeing the alarm with a hint of concern. Precision is great for training and running a tight ship as the director of player development for the New Jersey Devils. It's not so great for drawing out stories and insight for a book. Duggan, you should probably know or maybe already guessed, is very type A. She's always been. The youngest of three children, she was the most strong-willed of the Duggan kids, from what she wore to the sports she played.

"She was so loud," her dad, Bob Duggan, said. "People used to comment, in a multi-rink facility, all they had to do was listen and they knew where they were playing. She was yelling at everyone."

The same went for baseball. And lacrosse. She's so type A, she can still remember the one time she was late for something. That's how much it affected her. The U.S. national women's team was playing in the 2011 World Championships in Ottawa. Rooming with Kacey Bellamy, they were taking their post-breakfast nap when the phone rang. It was the general manager of the team, wondering where they were.

"We were like, 'Fuuuuuuuucck,'" she said. "I'm such a big believer in that details matter so much."

Precision. Attention to details. Setting an alarm for 1:27 p.m. so that a single minute isn't wasted. Part of it is how she's wired, how she was born. The other part spawned from one of the lowest moments of her life, heightening an obsession that drove her into one of the most impressive four years in the history of women's sports.

The sound that came from Meghan Duggan when she saw her parents outside Sochi's Bolshoy Ice Dome in 2014 was guttural. It was a cry of anguish so crushing and memorable, one observer said they can still hear it when they close their eyes and think of that moment. It was so different than the yell she let out earlier that day in celebration of her goal that gave Team USA an early 1–0 lead against Team Canada in the second period of their Olympic gold medal game. That one was pure joy. She had just buried a shot that exemplified everything about her. It was timely. It was precise. Placed in the only location that could beat the goalie. She dropped to one knee in celebration before being quickly wrapped up in a hug by Bellamy. The lead would build to 2–0 when Alex Carpenter scored on the power play early in the third period for the Americans.

Hockey Canada had won three consecutive Olympic gold medals in women's hockey, including one four years earlier in which a younger Meghan Duggan had to watch as the Canadian women smoked victory cigars on their home Vancouver ice in Duggan's first-ever trip to the Olympics. It hurt, but for her it was a learning experience. She suspected she'd have another crack at it.

After that loss in Vancouver, Duggan's close friend and Olympic teammate in 2010, Erika Lawler, remembers Team USA captain Natalie Darwitz talking about the pressures that came with the captaincy of an Olympic team.

"She was like, 'Man, I can't even explain how to be captain of that team,'" Lawler said. "You have to make so many decisions in an emotional state. You have a whole team to think about. It's just a lot to be a captain. A lot of your energy is drained on things that aren't hockey. Your energy just gets swept away."

Lawler would see it happen to her friend when, a year later, that responsibility fell to Duggan. A couple of days before the 2011 Four Nations tournament in Sweden, Duggan was named the captain of the women's national team. She was twenty-four. In that tournament, Duggan and her teammates would win gold, beating Canada. When she returned to the Olympics for the second time, in 2014, she returned as the leader of the team, one loaded with young talent.

"They had a clear advantage over Canada. '14 was their year," Lawler said. "They were just so good."

As the clock closed in on the final buzzer against Canada in Sochi, it started to feel like Duggan had turned in the perfect performance as captain. A crucial goal. Defending a shutout in one of sport's best rivalries. The first American Olympic hockey gold medal since 1998 was minutes away. Then Canada scored on a fluky goal that ricocheted off Bellamy's leg to cut the Americans' lead to one with 3:26 left in the game. Still, the great teams find a way to win even in those moments. When Team USA's Kelli Stack shot the puck the length of the ice, with Canada's goal empty for the extra attacker, this looked like one of those moments that seal it. It was a great shot, really, from the opposing blue line with a Canadian in her face pressuring her.

"It's going all the way down the ice, we're talking gold medal on the line," Duggan said, reliving the moment years later. "It hits the post and just stops right in the crease and just sits there. Not hits the post and goes in or goes in the corner. It sits there. And those types of things, they haunt you."

When Canada coach Kevin Dineen called a time-out, his group had just seventy-four seconds to tie the game. Canadian legend Marie-Philip Poulin needed only twenty of them, scoring a goal just out of the reach of the defending Duggan. Again, the difference between gold and silver measured in inches. Years later, Bellamy would describe the feeling in the Team USA dressing room heading into overtime as a group pretending to be confident. Duggan put the feeling much more bluntly: "Imagine that locker room. We're going to fucking lose this game."

Poulin, again, did the formalities, delivering the dagger of inevitability to finish the comeback and finish off the Americans. After the medals were awarded, the anthem played, the flags raised, families waited outside to pick up the pieces. Perhaps the cruelest thing about losing an Olympic gold medal game in women's hockey is that you have to wait four excruciating years for redemption. Four years to think about how close the gold was. Four years to torture yourself with what-ifs.

"It sounds crazy and now my perspective has changed since I've had kids, but the loss in Sochi was life-altering for me," Duggan said. "Completely life-altering. I took it personally."

Bob and Mary Duggan waited for their daughter outside the arena, surrounded by the darkness of the evening, unsure exactly which of the doors she might emerge from. As a parent, there's no preparing for this, no explaining the sound of anguish that comes from your child in a moment like this. All you can do is hold them when they collapse.

"She fell into my wife's and my arms," Bob Duggan said. "She was a mess. A complete mess. It took her a while for her to get over it. Honestly, I think it stuck with her. You don't get over that loss. She was devastated."

This is the origin story of the Meghan Duggan you see now.

The one obsessed with details. With precision. The one who, when our second interview wrapped up, jogged out of the room to her next scheduled event. She doesn't waste a minute because whatever is accomplished in that minute might be the difference between success and failure. It's what happens when you lose everything you've worked for by one inch. In order to beat Canada four years later in the Olympics, she understood that she didn't just have to find another gear in her preparation. She had to convince the entire roster to find that same drive. To do things completely differently.

"I vowed to myself that I would do literally everything I could possible to lead our team to the gold medal in 2018," Duggan said. "And one of our mottos as a team was you can't stay the same and expect a different result. That's what we did with everything. It wasn't easy at the time. I made a lot of enemies along the way, pushing people where they didn't want to be pushed, pushing myself where I didn't want to be pushed. The end goal was to win. To be perfect."

She didn't know it when she set out to win gold in 2018, but perfection also included one more small thing: a complete transformation of the way women's hockey players were treated in the United States, which would require her to take a stand as captain that could have cost her everything.

———————————

Four years.

It can be a transformative stretch of time. It's the time between a freshman walking through the doors of a school and leaving in a cap and gown, a completely different person. It's an American president, showing up at inauguration full of promise and leaving with a head full of gray hair. Four years. Do it right and you can change everything.

From 2015 to 2018, as captain of the women's U.S. national team, Duggan had to completely change how her team prepared for Canada. They'd lost four consecutive Olympic gold medal games. The same preparation wasn't going to work. And it meant getting everybody involved. To leave a lasting legacy, it had to be everybody.

"This is why Meghan is such a tremendous leader," said Reagan Carey, who was director of women's hockey at USA Hockey from 2010 to 2022. "She wasn't just the captain of our national team, she was the captain of our entire program."

This would surface in a critical way later in this four-year stretch.

But first, she set the tone early on in the training process.

The first summer after those crushing Olympics, sixty-six of the most talented girls' hockey players in America gathered at a U18 camp at the University of New England, in Biddeford, Maine. A few players from the 2014 Olympic team showed up to help out, pass on knowledge, and set expectations. Carey asked the Olympians to address the girls. Because she trusted the leadership instincts of the veterans—Meghan Duggan, Kacey Bellamy, Brianna Decker, among others—she didn't give them any specifics on what she wanted them to tell the team. She was just as curious as all the girls were, gathered in a room above the rink, when the room got dark and the crushing gold medal game against Canada from Sochi flickered on the screen in front of everyone. For most of those who were at home watching in 2014, cheering on their mentors, this was the first time they'd watch the replay. For the women who played in it, who suffered the gut-wrenching loss, it was the first time they'd rewatch it, too.

After that loss, they heard from all the well-meaning people who came up to them and told them the Canadians got lucky. That one bounce the right way would have changed everything. That it wasn't their fault, it was just some cruel management of fate by the hockey gods. Hear it enough and you can start to believe it. Duggan and the leadership group decided not to believe it. They decided to own it.

Own the loss.

It started by watching the game again in front of a room full of the next generation of players. As the game progressed, the U18 players hung on every play. That shot down the ice from Kelli Stack still hit the post. It still just sat there. It's never going to go in, no matter how many times you watch this game. When it was done, the lights came on. The women in the room who played in that game pulled out their silver Olympic medals and passed them around the room. The players felt them. They turned them over. They stared at the silver.

When everyone had a chance to touch the Olympic medals, Duggan walked to the front of the room.

"Did everyone have a chance to hold it?" she asked of the silver medals.

Everybody nodded.

"Great. That's the last time anybody is going to touch a silver medal in our program again."

Carey can still remember the way she felt standing in the room as Duggan delivered that message. The electricity. The determination.

"From that moment on, our U18 team or our national team all went undefeated in [International Ice Hockey Federation] competitions all the way through the Olympics," Carey said. "Talk about putting it out there. Owning it. . . . She was the essential multigenerational backbone of the program."

To get there, they believed they had to change everything, and Duggan, fair or not, believed that burden fell on her. Amanda Pelkey lived with Duggan during this time as she evolved as a leader. She saw how relentless she was in her pursuit of making the next day better. How she was in bed by 8:30 p.m. so she could wake up early to get in the right frame of mind for training.

"I would walk out in the living room—she was always up way before me, drinking coffee. She looked like she wasn't really there," Pelkey said. "You'd look at her and she was in the zone already. We weren't starting training for another two hours."

The mandate from management and coaches was that the 2018 Olympic team was going to be the fastest one the Americans ever sent to the games. That meant they had to ramp up their off-ice work. They brought in Jim Radcliffe, the head strength and conditioning coach at the University of Oregon, to revamp their training. The thought process was simple: if you want to play fast, you have to train fast. They also wanted to play with the puck. The team would gather at camps and watch old film of the Soviet Union's Red Army hockey team. Valeri Kharlamov to Vladimir Petrov to Boris Mikhailov to Slava Fetisov. Then it became film of the famed Russian Five, to watch the next generation of Russians do the same thing for the Detroit Red Wings. Sergei Fedorov to Slava Kozlov to Igor Larionov.

They'd watch and they'd emulate. How the Soviets refused to give up possession of the puck. How they always seemed to know where one another were on the ice, playing as a group of five.

"In all those years, we maybe dumped the puck in five times," Pelkey said. "I personally loved playing that way."

But the most transformative work was on the mental side. These are the best hockey players in the world. They've done everything imaginable on the ice to get better. Mental strength is where they believed they needed to close the gap most against Canada. Dr. Colleen Hacker had worked with the U.S. Women's National Soccer Team for twelve years. She was part of the team that won the historic 1999 World Cup. She won soccer Olympic gold medals in 2004 and 2008. She has been inducted into seven Halls of Fame as a player and coach. When Carey called her to work with the women's national hockey team, she said she was retired. That soon changed.

"She was a huge piece of our imagery, our visualization, performance anxiety," Duggan said. "We spent four years preparing for what [the gold medal game] would feel like. We spent four years preparing—'You're down, two to zero, to Canada in a gold medal game. There's seven minutes left. What are you going to do? Are you going to be like, "I can't believe this is happening again?" Marie-Philip Poulin scores a goal to put Canada up. What are you going to do?'"

The players would spend time every single day closing their eyes and training their bodies to experience the feeling of what the gold medal game in South Korea would feel like. What would it smell like on the ice? How would it sound? The players carried journals. Days on the ice were followed by weight lifting and then extended into quiet sessions outside the rink putting thoughts onto paper. Players would ask Duggan, what should I write? Is it supposed to be a paragraph? A page?

There wasn't a right answer.

Just write one word. Write three words. Scribble something on the pages.

At one point, the coaching staff gathered the team for practice and instead of sending them on the ice, sent them up into the stands. They would still practice, but it was all going to be done in their heads, with their eyes closed. Not on the ice.

"We would be sitting there with our eyes closed for forty-five minutes," Pelkey said.

Practicing.

Not every idea was great. The blindfolded session on the ice, for instance. And as you might guess, there was grumbling. Why are we doing this? What does it accomplish? How are imagined practices going to help beat Canada? Duggan pushed them through it. This was a team full of stars, with different personalities. Different ways of doing things. Different ways of seeing things. There was no better example of that difference than Hilary Knight, perhaps the player who will go down as the best to ever play the women's game in the United States. She was also someone who wasn't afraid to challenge Duggan.

"We saw things differently all the time, our careers," Duggan said. "We had this relationship where we could challenge each other, battle it out, be pissed off at each other, but we had a deep-rooted relationship where we could help the team and make it work."

Duggan continued.

"You hear all these stories where guys will fight in practice and they'll beat each other up in the locker room and then they're best buddies that night, right? It doesn't always happen on the women's side. . . . We believed in each other in terms of what all our end goal and focus was. Sometimes we had different paths to get there and that's when we challenged each other, but at the end of the day, it always came back to the team.

"We didn't just show up at the rink and float through our

days. We showed up at the rink and challenged each other. Did we do this? Did we prepare like that? What are we doing at practice today? We beat each other up on the ice, we called each other out when there were things people shouldn't have been doing, but all with the same end goal in mind. But it was hard. . . . It's hard to change people. It's hard to change people and convince people to try something new and different. It was hard for me. It was hard to lead a group that way."

Kacey Bellamy remembered one on-ice training session that Duggan was running. They were doing sprints on the ice and Bellamy was being pushed beyond what her body was accepting.

"The rest-work ratio was zero," Bellamy said. "I'm dying by the fifth one."

Duggan kept pushing until Bellamy finally yelled at her across the ice. She'd had enough.

"It's hard," Bellamy shouted.

Duggan yelled back.

"If it were easy, we'd have two more gold medals right now."

They kept skating.

———

Johnette Howard has been covering women's sports from the start of Title IX through the launch of professional sports leagues with franchises worth millions. She's worked for *Sports Illustrated* and ESPN. She's written a book with Billie Jean King. In this four-year window, she talked to Duggan a lot. She's not exactly sure when she posed the question, but she remembers the answer distinctly.

"Do you think people underestimate the will of world-class athletes?" Howard asked.

"All the time," Duggan answered.

In her time covering sports, Howard came to believe that it's magnified even more with world-class women athletes.

"There are just some things women know. You're kind of used to being ritually underestimated," Howard said. "You kind of keep your mouth shut. You're sort of used to it. It kind of turns to your advantage. You're always observing people and how they behave. And they always reveal themselves."

Howard added one more observation.

"The other lesson across women's sports—you have to go build it yourself," she said. "Nobody is going to do it for you. People are going to tell you that you can't. You won't. That nobody cares. They always get proven wrong."

These two beliefs would end up playing an important part of what Duggan and her teammates would accomplish off the ice in those four years. There's a power that comes with being underestimated. It pairs especially well with a group willing to stay united and do something themselves. In their federation, USA Hockey, the women found an adversary they believed underestimated their unified will.

In September 2016, the U.S. women's national team came together for a camp in Boston. The leaders of the team crammed into a hotel room to hear from Ballard Spahr lawyers John Langel and Dee Spagnuolo for the first time in person. It was Langel who identified the 2017 World Championships in Plymouth, Michigan, as the point at which these women would have the most leverage against USA Hockey in negotiations for equitable treatment. It was an important tournament at home. It was one year out from the Olympics.

The national team and USA Hockey had quietly been having negotiations since 2015 to close the gap between how women were treated compared to men by USA Hockey. They had no shortage of examples of preferential treatment for the men. There was the $15 per diem the women got during events compared to $50 for the men. It was superstar Hilary Knight squeezing into the last row of coach on a flight home from a tournament while the men flew first class. It was the goalies entering international tournaments representing their country while wearing pads in the school colors of their colleges, since they weren't provided equipment. There was the request to get paid in between Olympic Games while training as members of the national team that got this response: nobody is making the training mandatory.

It was also about money. According to ESPN, the women on the national team were only paid $6,000 by USA Hockey for the six-month residency leading up to the Olympic Games. That was the only money paid by the federation to the women in between epic Olympic gold medal battles with Canada. They also received small training stipends from the United States Olympic Committee.

In their book *Dare to Make History,* Jocelyne and Monique Lamoureux wrote that USA Hockey brought in $43 million in revenue in 2014. They only spent $1 million of it on the women's national team, the jewel of the program based on their accomplishments.

In an indication that the will of these women was being underestimated, Duggan said she noticed USA Hockey officials nodding off during meetings.

"We met with them all the time for a year and a half," she said. "Those meetings were almost harder because they just kept dismissing us and falling asleep in meetings."

It was during the meeting in Boston, with players crammed

into a hotel room talking to their lawyers, where it became apparent that a boycott that seemed like a long shot might become a necessity.

"There was a long period of time where I thought to myself that it is so far away, there's no way they'll let us get to that point. There was this denial that we're not going to have to get there. To me, it started to come into clear sight probably in the six months or so leading up," Duggan said. "We were meeting with USA Hockey, they would tell us one thing and not follow up. Our meetings were just going nowhere. Such a waste of time."

Cammi Granato was in Florida with her kids on spring break when she saw the news that the women were publicly boycotting the World Championships unless the two sides came to a new agreement. She'd been in regular communication with Duggan throughout the process, offering her advice and support, so it wasn't surprising. But still. To see what had been happening behind closed doors for years come to the public light in such a meaningful way, and then to be supported so strongly by sports fans, struck Granato.

"These girls are amazing. They are doing it. They all have the courage to do it. They're all banded together," Granato remembered thinking.

While the press releases and all the public appearances made by Duggan and her teammates talked about fighting this fight for women and girls in the future, there was also motivation from the past. A couple of years after winning gold with Team USA in the 1998 Winter Olympics, Granato and her teammates met with American gold medalists from other sports, including the U.S. women's soccer team. They hung out with them for a weekend in California and talked about how the women's soccer team's fight for equality was something the hockey program could emulate.

"They were like, 'You guys should be fighting for your rights.' It opened our eyes that they were able to get a few things by standing up for themselves. I think, at that point, our team was like, 'We're in,'" Granato said.

They connected with Ballard Spahr, the same law firm Duggan and her teammates would use years later. As a group, they wrote a letter to USA Hockey stating the things they believed they needed to compete. The response wasn't ideal. If they were looking for support or engagement, they weren't going to get it. Their requests were met with anger and indignation.

"It literally just blew up into anger from USA Hockey and our coaching staff. I'll never forget the call I got from [Team USA coach] Ben Smith, livid." Granato said. "We couldn't understand, didn't realize how we'd be received. We're literally just talking here. They were so unbelievably offended."

Granato's attempt to stand up for her rights and those of her teammates severed a bond that had just a few years earlier been completely historic when she helped the program win a gold medal in the first women's Olympic hockey tournament.

"It was a game changer," Granato said. "It severed a tie between us and USA Hockey."

In September 2005, Smith cut Granato from the team preparing for the Olympics. When she was cut, she was the all-time leading scorer in women's hockey during international competition, with 177 goals in 191 games. At the time, Smith told the *Denver Post* that it was a difficult decision but that "we have to pick the best opportunity for success." She was battling through a knee injury, but it doesn't take a leap to draw a connection between her shocking end to national team play and attempts to fight for equality.

"In the end, there wasn't a trust there. In the end, I think I was cut for who knows what reason, to be honest," she said. "There was no communication. It was a different time."

Duggan isn't so diplomatic.

"Yes, I think she was probably cut because she was a really strong, influential personality in terms of trying to fight for what was right," Duggan said.

That's what was on the line in this fight in 2017. All of these women saw what happened to the generation before them when icons in American hockey tried to do the same thing. Immediately after the boycott was announced, USA Hockey worked to replace the women on the national team.

The boycott was announced on Wednesday, March 15. The World Championships on home soil were scheduled to start on March 31. Quickly, it became a race to connect with every eligible women's hockey player in the United States to make sure they were all fighting the same fight. The Duggan family has a room in the back of their home with an office desk, and Bob Duggan remembers his daughter working frantically for hours populating a spreadsheet with contact information and then reaching out to anybody who USA Hockey might try to get to break the boycott.

"I remember her going, 'I'm going to make the phone call to every single person. I think it's important they hear from me.' I thought, 'Wow, that sums her up.' Not that she can't delegate, but 'this is really important they hear from me,' the willingness to have those conversations, the willingness to 'take fifty hours of my time to do this,'" said her wife, Gillian Apps. "It's for the next generation that's coming or girls in the next Olympic cycle. . . . It was impressive. I had never seen anything like that behind the scenes."

"We didn't want to strong-arm anyone," Duggan said. "We wanted to say, 'This is what we're doing. This is how it's evolved. This is why we're doing it. . . . We're just asking you to take a stand with us if you believe in it.' We just worked the phones for like three days. It was insane."

These weren't easy phone calls. A younger player might get a call from the coaching staff offering them a shot to play on their first-ever World Championship team and then the next call would be from Duggan asking them not to accept. Or it was getting parents on speakerphone so they knew exactly what their kid was giving up as they went down the depth charts.

"How do you convince parents who want nothing more than their daughter to get the call-up for the national team—how do you convince them? I don't know how she did it," said former teammate and close friend Erika Lawler. "That was just insane to me, to wrap my head around. It's so hard to get buy-in. . . . That speaks to how much respect she had garnered."

In the end, the women and girls were united. USA Hockey officials were reaching out to players at the lowest levels of college hockey and still not getting commitments. Often, Duggan or a teammate had already beaten them to the conversation.

On Monday, March 20, five days after the boycott became public and eleven days before they were scheduled to play Canada in the World Championships, the two sides met at the Ballard Spahr offices. At this point, the story was a national media sensation. Duggan's phone was buzzing constantly with interview requests. As the women entered the law firm, there were cameras out front to record their entrance. Any pleasantries that might have accompanied previous talks were gone. After about eight hours of stalled negotiations, the two sides agreed to break into separate rooms and work on counteroffers that might move the talks forward. Until that point, the lawyers did most of the speaking for the women.

During the break, Duggan spoke up.

For the first time during this boycott she felt a weariness from her teammates. People were getting tired. There was definitely a vibe of "When are we going to be done with this?" Just like she might push a teammate for extra sprints on the ice, she asked for her teammates to dig in even more.

Take a deep breath and buckle up. We're not rolling over. This is the language we should choose. This is how we should approach this. These are the exact examples we should give and why we're so passionate about it.

Langel watched as she delivered this message to teammates.

"I think you should be the one to say it to them," he said.

Langel appreciated her emotion, how she was willing to leave this conversation without a deal. USA Hockey needed to hear that from the captain of the women's national team. They re-entered the room. Duggan remembered it being a beautiful space. A huge rectangular table in the middle. Large glass windows all around. On one side of the table were people who had once supported them in tournaments, like executive director Dave Ogrean, president Jim Smith, and general counsel Casey Jorgensen. Her teammates were on the other side, with even more on a conference call listening in. Dedicated women in places like California and Minnesota who couldn't be there in person, but who sat and listened to hours and hours of conversations. She shared the message she told her teammates on break. They weren't backing down. They would leave without a deal if they had to.

"I was probably not super emotional, but visibly amped up. I was passionate about this," she said. "I would like to think they were looking at me thinking this is a well-respected person in our program and captain. This is how she feels. It's not just these women whining through lawyers. This is real and this is our life."

A handshake deal was made. The session went so long that all the players missed their evening flights and needed to visit a local Target and load up on sweatpants, T-shirts, and toothbrushes to get through a surprise stay in Philadelphia. Although tired, spirits were high as they worked through the Target aisles.

Then the deal was rejected by USA Hockey's executive committee.

On Monday, March 27, the week of the World Championships, twenty United States senators sent a letter to USA Hockey saying the women "deserve fairness and respect." USA Hockey's board of directors organized an emergency conference call and, as it turns out, Duggan was on the board call because of her position as an athlete director. At the outset of the call, she made a point of letting people know she was on the call and leading the other side. She also got about ninety seconds to state her case and explain the stance the women were taking. Then she listened in as she said their demands and point of view were completely mischaracterized.

"The numbers and the way things were presented from USA Hockey were false. They were presenting it to their own board and fabricating things," Duggan said. "I said, 'Guys, I'm a player living this every single day. We're not being compensated at all. One dollar. I don't know where you're getting those numbers. They're false. I can tell you right now, none of this is accurate.'"

It was hard for her to listen to.

"There were a lot of people on the call prior to that I had respected and had great relationships with and was disappointed that they didn't stand with us when things got difficult," Duggan said.

Cammi Granato was also on the call, and this was the moment, for her, that Duggan's leadership was on full display.

"There were people coming at her. She was unbelievable with handling the pressure with that situation, that many people on the line," Granato said. "It was not a happy group. I knew from how we were dealt with, which was basically like, 'You just severed your ties and you're going to pay.' It was like a vengeance against us. I'm listening to her standing up to this group and I'm thinking, 'She's killing it. She's not backing down.'"

The call ultimately led to an agreement the next day. Johnette Howard had all the details on ESPN.com, details that included an annual compensation of roughly $70,000 per player, with performance bonuses tied to success at the Olympics and World Championships that could push it even higher, like $20,000 for a gold medal. There were travel benefits and insurance that was on par with the men. There would be a new committee established to help promote the women's game. There was a foundation position created to help with its girls' developmental teams. Duggan remembers getting the term sheet on her phone in her apartment. It was a one-sheeter with the broad strokes for the lawyers to dive into. She signed it. Almost immediately, the itinerary for a flight to Detroit, Michigan, was sent to her email from USA Hockey.

They had a game with Canada in two days.

"It was kind of the same feeling I had when I won the gold medal," said Kacey Bellamy of ending the boycott with a clear victory. "This euphoric feeling of pride, historic, 'We did this.' And then, if you knew our team back then and that leadership, it was 'Now we have a job to do.'"

That job started with a gold medal in the 2017 World Championships. But the bigger assignment was still to come.

———————————

The first time Ray Shero met Meghan Duggan was at the 2014 Winter Olympics in Sochi. He was part of the management group for the men's team, where he roomed with Brian Burke in the Olympic Village. The women's team was staying a few floors down, so the two teams would cross paths in common areas. His first impression was from running into her in the training room, where she was getting treatment.

"Her thigh was black, purple, orange, everything," Shero said. "Holy shit."

His next impression was just how crushed the women were after losing to Canada in the gold medal game. There was no hiding in the Olympic Village and he saw a team absolutely devastated. The men also lost a close game to Canada and then got blown out, 5–0, to Finland in the bronze medal game. It was a rough way to finish their tournament. But Shero remembered thinking that the men could go back to the NHL, back into playoff races, and quickly move on from their disappointment. Team USA goalie Jonathan Quick, for instance, would raise a Stanley Cup above his head a few months later in pure elation after leading the Los Angeles Kings to a championship. The women had to wait four years for redemption.

"I always had a lot of respect for the women and what they put into it," Shero said.

Shero is also a connector. He's quick to help people network in the game and knows nearly everybody. So he was sincere when he approached Duggan at some point after those games and offered to help her pursue a career in the NHL whenever she was done playing.

That moment came in October of 2020. She spent the first few months after retiring as a player with her family, but was thinking about what came next. She grew up a Boston Bruins fan and always had a dream of working in the NHL. So she started building out a contact list of people she'd come across through the years who were working in the NHL. People who worked for the league. In marketing. In front offices. In coaching. When you're an Olympian there's no shortage of people offering to connect. Duggan was ready to cash in on those offers and she started with Shero.

"I just reached out and said, 'Hey, Ray, you were one of the mentors who was just so open to connecting.' I said, 'I'm looking to get involved in men's pro hockey and would love to pick your brain about ways I can build my resume,'" Duggan said.

Shero remembered the conversation. He offered to connect her with anyone in his circle she wanted to talk to.

"I'll never forget what she said," Shero said. "She said, 'Ray, no one is going to want to talk to me.' I was like, 'Meghan, are you serious?'"

He reached out to Burke. He reached out to Jason Botterill. He reached out to Tom Fitzgerald. The response was always the same when the request went out to talk to Duggan. Of course.

The most important connection might have been with Kate Madigan. Madigan had been hired by the New Jersey Devils in 2017 as an assistant working with player information and video. Before that she was an audit assistant at the accounting firm Deloitte & Touche. Shero explained the situation to Madigan, pointing out that they were both from Massachusetts. Duggan and Madigan spoke for forty-five minutes and it was all the time Madigan needed. Her next call was to Devils GM Tom Fitzgerald.

"I went to Fitzy and said, 'We're hiring her,'" Madigan said. "He said, 'We don't have a job.' I said, 'Figure it out.'"

What stood out in those forty-five minutes?

"She's awesome. I can't explain it. She has high IQ and EQ, which is hard," Madigan said.

Fitzgerald wanted more examples of what made Madigan so convinced Duggan should be offered a job on the spot.

"Just talk to her," Madigan answered.

He did. He walked away just as convinced.

"The fire. The passion. The enthusiasm," Fitzgerald said. "I didn't watch her play all that much, but what I've been told is she'll chop your leg off if it meant getting the puck from you. Her competitiveness is off the charts. You see it in her passion."

In May of 2021, the Devils made it official. They hired her as manager of player development, making her the first openly gay person to work in an NHL front office. One year later, she was promoted to director of player development. An NHL front office hiring a former player isn't particularly noteworthy, but Fitzgerald quickly discovered the benefits of hiring a player from the women's side of the hockey world. One of the things former NHL players struggle with in retirement is the lack of structure. There isn't someone scheduling their day. There isn't a team services director planning meals or travel. The women, while training on their own between big events, learn time management. They learn how to plan everything. When the women's national team boycotted USA Hockey, it was the players who did the graphic design for social media posts. Duggan was setting up spreadsheets and conference calls.

"Talk about self-sufficient, the women have raised themselves in their own game to do everything," Fitzgerald said. "I was hiring someone unique . . . very self-sufficient. Very precise. Very on task. It was like, 'I don't have to worry about this. It's in great hands.'"

Factor in her ability to play hockey at the highest level in the world and the Devils quickly realized they had something special. A few minutes after Fitzgerald and I were done talking, we both walked around the corner to a spot above the stands overlooking the Devils practice rink. The stands were jammed with Devils fans looking to get a hockey fix on a warm mid-July evening. The sheet of ice had been divided into three sections, with games of three-on-three between Devils prospects being played simultaneously on either end. In the center section, players waited for their shift, surrounded by coaches.

Duggan, of course, was in the middle of it. She was skating from player to player, pulling them aside. She had a stick in her hand. At one point, she gathered a group of players, and after instructing them for a few minutes, she said something and they all let out a big laugh.

"She can really relate to these kids," Fitzgerald said. "They respect the shit out of her. They really do. And her peers within the hockey community, people who work for her and are above her, there's just utmost respect. I'm going to lose her someday to be a GM. She's already interviewed for a GM job. I know it's going to happen."

A few months earlier, the Pittsburgh Penguins interviewed Duggan for their vacant general manager job just two years into her tenure as an NHL executive. The first thing she did—before calling her wife, before calling her parents—was to call Cammi

Granato, now an assistant GM with the Vancouver Canucks. Granato had guided her through so much. First as a trailblazer in the sport, later as an inspiration and guide in the fight for equality, and now as an NHL colleague.

"You go and try and get this," Granato told her. "This isn't just an experience of going through the process. Realize you're capable."

Duggan didn't get it. Neither did her Devils front office teammate Kate Madigan, who also interviewed. Shortly after that process, the NHL world congregated in Nashville for the 2023 draft. There was a Women in Hockey Operations happy hour one of the evenings before the draft. When Madigan and Duggan and Granato gathered on a patio at 1 Hotel Nashville for a photo to mark the night, more than thirty women squeezed in, the first two rows kneeling on gray granite to make room for everyone. It's still a number that was dwarfed by the men on the draft floor later that week, but it was progress.

"It was really cool to just look around and see how many women were represented at the draft and were there representing all the different teams," Granato said.

But more important, she said, is that the men who work with the women in the group understand their worth to the organization.

"As soon as they start working with you, it's not about gender anymore," Granato said. "It's how you can do it."

—————————————————

On Thursday, February 22, 2018, at the Gangneung Hockey Centre in South Korea, Duggan and the U.S. women's national team found itself tied once again with Canada in an Olympic gold medal game. Each team had two goals after three periods of play. It was the exact same situation they found themselves in four years earlier in Sochi. But somehow completely different. They had years of mental training. Hours of imagining this exact moment. They had been through so much as a group together.

"It's pretty incredible to think about. Replaying both of these games in my head. It's a different mentality in both and that's the difference," said Kacey Bellamy. "[2014] was complete silence and we pretended to be confident. The next one, we were still laughing and having fun in the locker room, but you had the serious nature of 'We're going to get it done.' That's the biggest difference. We had no doubts in 2018."

Overtime started with the two teams playing tentatively until the Americans started to turn up the pressure. Accompanied by chants of "USA! USA! USA!" the women peppered what looked like a tiring Canadian defense until longtime nemesis Marie-Philip Poulin remarkably drew a penalty with 1:35 remaining in overtime. It was frantic, and one shot passed through the crease during those final ninety-five seconds of four-on-three, but the clock hit zero and it was down to a shootout. Four years of work, sweat, tears, fights, boycotts, journals, blindfolds, sprints, and pain not only came down to the shootout, it came down to sudden death in the shootout after the score was even following five rounds.

Maybe you've seen it: Jocelyne Lamoureux swerving slowly down the ice, dekeing, then flashing the blade of her stick, dekeing again, before slicing it behind Canadian goalie Shannon Szabados to put Team USA one save away from their first gold medal in women's Olympic hockey in twenty years. And, moments later, that one save being made by goalie Maddie Rooney on Meghan Agosta, followed immediately by the Americans tossing gloves and sticks in the air in pure jubilation as they won the gold medal. It was an amazing moment for these women.

Maybe you even saw Duggan clutching an American flag in one hand, hugging one teammate after another tightly in celebration as tears ran down the cheeks of both the celebrating Americans and devastated Canadians watching on the bench. Maybe you saw Team USA taking a team photo on the ice while singing along with "Don't Stop Believin'" as it echoed over the arena's speakers. Or 1998 gold medal winner Angela Ruggiero placing Duggan's first Olympic gold medal around her neck, something new to show the next group of kids at a U18 camp in Maine.

But only her former roommate and teammate, Amanda Pelkey, witnessed a moment that she'd get emotional retelling years later. As the players partied, their friends and families exited the arena. Instead of waiting outside the rink like they did four years earlier to catch devastated loved ones in their arms, they found a nearby pub to celebrate and wait.

Eventually the players made their way to join up for celebratory drinks and dinner. Pelkey was directly behind Duggan as she walked up the stairs toward the waiting party. There were friends and family on the right and left at the top of the stairs.

Standing in front at the top was Meghan's wife, Gillian Apps. Apps had won three gold medals for Canada, so she knew exactly what Duggan was feeling. But more than anyone, she knew what Duggan had gone through to get to that moment. Duggan, who never let her guard down for anyone publicly, did for Apps.

"She obviously saw those little cracks," Pelkey said. "She saw everything, being her person."

And for a moment, Pelkey said, everything went black.

It was just Meghan and Gillian.

Pelkey started crying. She knew the work, the sacrifice, even the abuse that Duggan took to get there. It all disappeared when Duggan was met at the top of those steps by her wife.

"To see that moment," Pelkey said, pausing, the emotions returning. "Nothing else mattered."

CHAPTER 6

THE ART OF LISTENING (AND MANAGING UP)

> Everybody is afraid to say it. There's nothing wrong with saying it. There's nothing wrong with saying you need to manage the person you report to and the people above them.
>
> **—Jim Rutherford**

We were on a patio overlooking the first tee of the Allegheny Country Club on an overcast June morning. The view was stunning, even on a gray day with a slight chill. It was cool enough that Jim Rutherford, sitting across from me at this outdoor table, ordered hot water with lemon as his drink. We were bordered by perfectly trimmed shrubs near an expanse of green rolling hills that eventually gave way to a tree line on the horizon.

It had been more than a few months since Rutherford shocked the hockey world by stepping down as the GM of the Pittsburgh Penguins, but he was still wearing Penguins gear, a black Adidas Penguins quarter zip to be exact. As he walked me through the country club, he shared the history of the club through the lens of which Penguins belong, most notably Mario Lemieux and Sidney Crosby. It would be another six months before Vancouver Canucks owner Francesco Aquilini would quietly fly down to Raleigh, North Carolina, to talk to Rutherford about becoming the president of the Canucks.

I caught him in between it all.

When Rutherford left the Pittsburgh Penguins in January 2021, he had been the general manager since the 2014–15 season. As the GM in Pittsburgh, he never missed the playoffs. He won back-to-back Stanley Cups in 2016 and 2017. He was inducted into the Hall of Fame in 2020. That success came off a twenty-year run with the Carolina Hurricanes franchise, which also included a Stanley Cup win, in 2006.

He made it clear on the day he resigned that it wasn't age-related. When the Associated Press called, he joked that the president at the time, Joe Biden, was much older than he was and his job much more stressful. Rutherford still wanted to work. He didn't resign because he wanted to golf, even if hole number one was inviting us to tee off. Even as we sat there, a rumor circulated that the Toronto Maple Leafs were interested in hiring him to help the front office. His phone was buzzing because of the speculation. At one point he looked down at a number calling him before sending it to voicemail.

"You know Dave Feschuk?"

"Yeah. He's in Toronto. He trying to get ahold of you?"

"They all are."

Here's the thing writers have learned about Jim Rutherford. If you get ahold of him, he's going to tell you what's going on. In his mind, people are going to write about his teams, so he might as well give them his version of the truth. In the early days of *The Athletic*, when every new subscription generated was tracked and celebrated, we used to encourage Penguins beat writer Josh Yohe to give Rutherford a call when business was slow. He usually delivered with a morsel of news that wasn't public. Then we'd count the new subscriptions.

As far as NHL general managers went, there were few as transparent.

"I'm not going to run to somebody and say, 'This is what we're doing.' But whoever the first call is—if they ask me the question, they're going to get the answer, okay?" Rutherford explained. "I think by giving the answer . . . I'm on record as saying what it is. I try to be truthful as possible. If I forget something, that's a different story."

It's what made the resignation such a stunner. He'd never hinted at it. There was no speculation about him wanting to leave the Penguins. On the day it happened, he came home and told his wife, Leslie, that he had resigned and that they should move back to Carolina. First there was shock. Then tears.

"It happened so fast," she said.

Over the next couple days, Rutherford heard from everyone. Texts. Phone calls. He expected to hear from a few people, but the sheer volume was twice as much as he ever imagined. People he hadn't heard from in years. Some in Pittsburgh he helped reach the highest mountaintop in hockey. When he read texts from Sidney Crosby and Evgeni Malkin, Leslie saw his eyes fill with tears.

"It meant a lot to me," Rutherford said. "It was almost like when somebody dies, when you go to the wake you say, 'God, he was a nice guy, really liked him,' or whatever they say. I got all those comments without dying."

Rutherford's honesty, his transparency brings that out of people. It's what makes the secrecy around the resignation so out of character. People certainly have their theories. There are some close to him who believe that Mario Lemieux tried to talk him out of it multiple times. In later conversations with the media, he would say that the toll of being isolated during COVID led to the decision. But if that's it, it would seem like an easy thing to say when we're chatting about it on this gray overcast June morning. Instead, when asked to discuss the decision, he declined.

"No. It's not going to do any good. It'd just give people something to talk about," he said. "I don't regret the decision. It was good it came at that time, that it gave enough time for someone else to get in there and do the work that was necessary for the season. No, they've been great to me here, I'm just thankful I got this opportunity. David Morehouse and ownership were really good to work with over those years. I had the same thing in Carolina. It was good to work with Pete [Karmanos]."

As we sat, Rutherford, sipping on chicken orzo soup between bites of a smoked salmon bagel, said he'd be content if his days as an NHL executive were finished. If he was done chasing another championship. The barrage of texts and calls he got after resigning was all the evidence he needed about his place in the game, about the respect he'd earned from the people he cares about. He was in the Hall. He had his three Cups.

"I don't have to have it," he said. "It's not like a drug."

But like his grandfather, who put in decades at the railroad, and his father on a used-car lot, he's a worker. He also likes trying to accomplish something, an opportunity that would present itself when Aquilini visited his home in Carolina six months after we met. And it's that drive to work that got him here in the first place.

Mark Craig had just lost a one-goal youth hockey game in Mich-igan with a 1980 state championship on the line, and as a young, competitive coach, he was upset. He didn't necessarily want to talk to the guy who walked up to him wearing jeans and a Pac-Man T-shirt after the game. The guy wanted to hire Craig to coach his team and was hoping to meet up with him to make the pitch. Eventually, they agreed to meet at the Golden Mushroom on 10 Mile Road in Southfield, Michigan, a restaurant known for its wild-game cuisine and a wine list with more than eight hundred options. Craig pulled into the parking lot, entered the restaurant, and settled down across the table from Peter Karmanos Jr.

Karmanos was the son of Greek immigrants and founder of Compuware, a software company he started shortly after leaving Wayne State University in Detroit. He was well on his way to massive business success and now had big ambitions in hockey. The conversation started with Karmanos explaining how he was going to build a local youth hockey powerhouse, then start hockey schools and manage arenas. After that, the plan was to buy an Ontario Hockey League junior team. And then an NHL fran-chise that would eventually win a Stanley Cup.

He wanted Craig to be a part of all of it.

"I go home and go, 'This guy is nuts. This guy is pure nuts,'" Craig said.

Maybe. But Karmanos wasn't giving up. After the meeting at the Golden Mushroom, Craig's wife let him know that a let-ter from Karmanos had arrived in the mail. It was a job offer. They quickly flipped through the letter to find the starting salary.

"She goes, 'You're going to take the job,'" Craig said. "That's how it started. What I realized with Pete is that this wasn't a dream. This was a plan. This guy had a plan. You start to realize he's going to make it happen. It didn't take me long to go, 'Oh shit, this guy is good.'"

So Craig started coaching the youth team. He started organizing hockey schools. The Karmanos hockey empire plan was in action. They just needed to find the person to bring it to the next level, a leader with NHL connections and the drive to match. In 1983, Jim Rutherford played his final season in the NHL. It was a professional career that started with him being the tenth overall selection in the 1969 draft. The day after that draft, Rutherford's mom and dad drove him down to the *Globe and Mail* to grab the first paper they could find that morning. It's how he discovered that he'd been picked by Detroit. Four or five days after the draft, the Red Wings called to see if their head scout could come up and visit Rutherford. When he arrived, he was armed with a $5,000 signing bonus and a contract that paid Rutherford $30,000 if he made it to the big club. Rutherford signed immediately. A year later, he embarked on a career that included more than four hundred NHL games in thirteen seasons with the Detroit Red Wings (three times), Pittsburgh Penguins, Toronto Maple Leafs, and Los Angeles Kings. He also popularized goalies painting their masks. It was a heck of a run for the son of a car salesman and grandson of a railroad worker. When he was done, Karmanos got word that Rutherford might be looking for a job in hockey and encouraged Craig to meet with him. They knew they could use him in their hockey schools, but suspected he could also be the connection that would help them land that OHL team.

After Rutherford was hired, Craig noticed that he showed

up everywhere, not just the goalie schools he was being paid to coach. He'd show up at squirt games. He'd show up at Craig's games. He was committed to getting involved, learning, and helping out. When Karmanos sat in the stands and watched how the goalie schools were being run, he also noticed Rutherford and his work ethic. After three days of watching Rutherford at one particular goalie school, Karmanos walked over to him while he was taking off his skates.

I like the way you work.

Rutherford thanked him.

No. Listen to me. I like the way you work.

Karmanos really wanted to drive home how impressed he was that Rutherford was willing to put in the kind of effort that he did as someone who had just been making six figures in the NHL. They met a few days later and Karmanos presented an offer. Work half the time at Compuware and the other half at the hockey schools. The pay? Twenty-four thousand dollars per year. Plus benefits. It was a massive pay cut for a former NHL player.

"I started the next day," he said.

Rutherford put in his time at Compuware trying to learn the software program. He was also working in the hockey schools. The software was complicated, but Rutherford made a go at it, and when Karmanos came to him after a couple of months and said he wanted him to shift all his energy toward growing the hockey empire, Rutherford suspected that the software portion was a test. Would he put in the work to try? Was he willing to try something new? Would he quit? If it was a test, Rutherford passed and was sent on to his next assignment: help Karmanos buy an OHL team. Rutherford met with OHL commissioner David Branch and learned that Windsor was headed for bankruptcy. It was perfect. Karmanos could get his team and live close enough to enjoy the games. Rutherford would run it as president and GM.

In the two seasons before Rutherford took over, the Spitfires won nineteen and twenty-two games, respectively. They played seventy each season. In 1984, Karmanos and the new ownership group took over, renamed them the Windsor Compuware Spitfires, and were playing for a Memorial Cup a few years later, putting up a 50–14–2 record en route to an OHL championship.

The awkward corporate name aside, the partnership was working. The group went from Windsor to launching an expansion team in Plymouth, Michigan, making them the first American-based team in the OHL. Then the focus shifted to the NHL and landing an expansion team there.

Rutherford moved to Florida to run point on a plan to bring an NHL franchise to St. Petersburg. The plan was to share space in what originally was called the Florida Suncoast Dome (now Tropicana Field). It's probably the worst ballpark in Major League Baseball and it's not much better for hockey. But for most of the expansion process of 1992, Karmanos, Rutherford, and the Trop were the favorites to land one of the two expansion slots. At some point Karmanos decided that he didn't feel it was the right business move to pay the entire $50 million expansion fee up front. Instead, he started floating the idea of paying a portion up front and the rest out of profits once the team was operational. The night before the expansion announcement, Rutherford and Karmanos went to a dinner at Bruins owner Jeremy Jacobs's house in West Palm Beach and Jacobs tried to convince Karmanos to just pony up the money so St. Petersburg could get the franchise.

"There are different owners coming up to Pete and I saying, 'Just pay the fifty,'" Rutherford said.

He never did, and the league held firm. Along with the St. Petersburg group, the NHL received applications from Tampa, Ottawa, Miami, Hamilton, San Diego, and Anaheim.

In return for a full $50 million expansion fee, Ottawa and Tampa brought the NHL's franchise count to twenty-four. A report in the *New York Times* hinted at the rivalry between Rutherford and Phil Esposito in landing one of these expansion slots, with Esposito scraping together last-minute financing from Japan to pull it off that included Esposito aggravating an old knee injury by trying to squeeze under a table in a Japanese tatami room.

"We didn't get the franchise, but the league was aware of our interest obviously and they made us aware of the Hartford situation," Rutherford said.

The lede on the Associated Press story from June 2, 1994, announcing the sale of the Hartford Whalers to Karmanos's group, gave the price tag ($47.5 million) and also the notion that the group does "intend to keep the team in Hartford for at least four years." Just over a decade after Rutherford was hired to work on software at Compuware for $24,000, he was running an NHL team. Just over a decade after Karmanos was sharing his vision with Craig at the Golden Mushroom about building his local youth hockey program into a hockey portfolio that included an NHL franchise, he now owned one. Three years later it was announced that the Hartford Whalers were moving to North Carolina.

Karmanos had his NHL franchise. He had his new NHL market. Everything he said he would do, he did. In the process, Rutherford learned how to get a deal done from a master. He learned how to execute a vision. How to be fearless in the pursuit of a deal. All lessons that would pay off with the same result for two different franchises.

It was late January in 2006 and the St. Louis Blues were strug-gling despite a talented roster. Doug Weight was nearly a point-per-game player. So was Keith Tkachuk. Barret Jackman and Eric Brewer anchored the defense. It was one of those teams that, if things fell the right way, you could see making a run. Things didn't fall the right way.

There was bickering in the locker room. Groups of players that didn't always get along. At one point in January, the Blues went nine straight games without a win. And even then, Weight wasn't sure he was ready to bail. So he called his agent, Steve Bartlett.

What do you think?

Your odds to get in the playoffs are two percent. And if you get in, do you think you're going to beat Colorado or Detroit?

Weight considered the question for a moment.

Let's get out of here.

Blues GM Larry Pleau asked Weight to meet at a Starbucks to make a plan. In the final year of his contract, Weight had a no-trade clause that allowed him control of the situation. Pleau and Weight sat down and went over the options. There were five or six teams interested in trading for Weight, but the best offers were from the Ottawa Senators and Carolina Hurricanes. This was an absolutely loaded Senators team making a push, a team that would finish with the most regular-season points in the East-ern Conference. Peak Jason Spezza, Dany Heatley, and Daniel Alfredsson Senators. The trade to Carolina came with a caveat from Rutherford communicated to Weight: Don't pick the Hur-ricanes if you're just trying to score a bunch of points. You're not going to get the same power play time. You're not coming in on the top line.

We're trying to win it all.

"I was like, 'Okay, I want to win,'" Weight said. "As long as they're not thinking of playing me every other game, I'm in. No matter what."

He liked that the Hurricanes were so up front with their intentions. That they put team success first. Yes, he had some concerns about their goaltending. He had no idea who the kid was backing up Martin Gerber, but he wasn't sweating it. He liked where he slotted in the lineup. He liked the idea of playing with Ray Whitney and Erik Cole.

"That's a no-brainer," Weight said.

So on a Monday in late January, Rutherford and Pleau made the deal. Rutherford paid a healthy price for a short-term rental, sending a first-round pick and two fourth-rounders along with a couple of players in return for Weight. But this is what Rutherford does. When he's ready to act, he sends a message and he usually does it early. He's done this time and time again with his teams, like his Vancouver Canucks did in acting decisively during the trade for Elias Lindholm well before the 2024 trade deadline.

"The biggest thing about that [Weight] deal, besides what he brought to the team, was the players started talking amongst themselves, 'God, they think we can win the Cup,'" Rutherford said. "And that started the momentum. That's when [coach] Peter [Laviolette] went to work and went in there and said, 'We can do this.'"

After his first game with the Hurricanes, Weight was working out when Rod Brind'Amour approached him. They chatted briefly about some of the rifts in the Blues dressing room and

Brind'Amour let him know they didn't have any of that in Carolina. He intended to keep it that way. He also reiterated what Rutherford said about Weight's role.

"I said, 'We're already really good, we're not going to all of a sudden find you twenty minutes. It's just not going to happen,'" Brind'Amour said. "He was great about it. You bring in guys like that and if they don't have the right attitude about it, they can actually take your team the other way."

When you see deadline deals go sideways despite the talent being added, that's often why. Sometimes it's players trying too hard to set up new teammates or their new teammates trying too hard to set them up. Or the new addition isn't happy with their new role on a better team. There's usually a long acclimation period and it's why Rutherford likes to strike early.

"He puts his finger on guys and he wants them and it's like, 'Why wouldn't I get him early for climatization factors? I'm going to give up another second-rounder? Who gives a shit? That's the guy,'" Weight said.

That's the guy.

And the reason Rutherford can make deal after deal, decade after decade, is that he isn't trying to win the deals. He actively wants the deal to work for both sides. He's even okay losing a few.

"Any GM who has made a trade with him will tell you this. He believes you can't make a lopsided trade and have it work out," Craig said. "It may work for you short term, but you're hurting yourself with that GM and other GMs. He's always told me that. From the early days in Windsor. You can't make trades where one guy doesn't get the right end."

Rutherford added Mark Recchi at the trade deadline for good measure and, of course, the Hurricanes won it all in 2006. Karmanos had his Stanley Cup championship just twenty-three years after telling the recently retired goalie that he liked the way he worked following a youth goalie camp. For a GM, it can be chaotic after winning a Cup. Because the offseason is short, there are roster decisions that have to be made immediately after the champagne is poured. There are lists to turn in—like who gets their name on the Cup and who doesn't. There's a draft to prepare for. But in the aftermath, Rutherford sat down and wrote Weight a letter. He thanked him for joining the Hurricanes, for putting the team first. For being part of the group that was the first professional team to bring a sports championship to North Carolina.

Weight hung it on his office wall, memorializing Rutherford's leadership.

"That meant a lot to me," Weight said. "It closed that era out."

When you think about the superpowers of some of the best leaders in sports, they often fall into categories. There's the offensive mastermind. There's the tactical genius. There are analytics experts and former players who have the charisma people naturally want to follow. Rutherford's biggest strength is something else completely.

When Cammi Granato joined the Vancouver Canucks as an assistant general manager, she only knew of Rutherford. Then she got to see him in action, and more than once she went home to her husband, Ray Ferraro, with the same report.

"I say this to Ray almost weekly. I love working for Jim. Every day you learn something," Granato said. "There's a greatness about him. It's this aura."

And what she's discovered, like so many before her, is that his superpower isn't something that you often hear at the top of the list of leader attributes. But maybe that's why it's so noteworthy. He's an incredible listener.

"Active listening," Granato said. "He's very selective with his words."

When Rutherford was running the Pittsburgh Penguins, he and coach Mike Sullivan had a running tradition they honored whenever the team left home. Sullivan and his coaching staff made a point of going out to dinner with Rutherford and anyone from hockey operations who was on the road with the team. These dinners were always good for a lot of laughs, and they were a way for everyone to get to know each other a little better, but the most valuable part, for Rutherford, was that they inevitably turned into conversations about hockey. And the Penguins. Why was the power play struggling? Which lines needed shaking up?

Sullivan said the same thing about Rutherford in those moments. He listened. During these conversations, he might offer a quick thought to spur the debate or let the coaches know of a player who might be available on the trade market. But mostly, he was there to get the pulse of the team. Along with a good meal.

"That's the one thing I've tried to learn from Jim and I apply with my coaches now is to have conversations and frame conversations in a way that you allow people to speak their minds and listen," Sullivan said. "You get valuable insights from other people around you when you have that modus operandi."

In the winter of 2016, Rutherford picked up on a theme during those dinners. The coaching staff wanted to get faster. They talked about the things they could do as a group with a little more speed. They discussed how they would implement a style of play if they just had the speed to do it.

"A lot of the seeds of those things started during informal conversations when we would spend time together on the road," Sullivan said.

Rutherford dropped the name Carl Hagelin into those conversations. The previous summer, Hagelin had been traded by the New York Rangers to the Anaheim Ducks in a deal for Emerson Etem. The Ducks signed him to a four-year contract worth $16 million. But he struggled to provide the offense the Ducks needed. He had just four goals in forty-three games with the Ducks and Rutherford knew he was available. He knew Ducks GM Bob Murray felt like Hagelin wasn't a fit on his team even if he had just signed him.

Rutherford had his own ill fit in David Perron, a player he spent a first-round pick to acquire from the Edmonton Oilers the previous year. Rutherford isn't afraid to admit a mistake and this was one of them. So he flipped Perron in a deal for Hagelin loaded with risk because of the term on Hagelin's contract and his lack of production with the Ducks. But because he knew exactly how his coaching staff would use him, how much they desired his speed, Rutherford was comfortable making that trade. It all fit together perfectly in eventually helping the Penguins form the HBK line—Hagelin, Nick Bonino, and Phil Kessel—all players acquired via trade by Rutherford.

The Penguins don't win back-to-back Stanley Cups without those deals.

Matt Cullen was a player through the years who got to know Rutherford well in both Carolina and Pittsburgh, and he singled out Rutherford's ability to identify exactly who is needed at the right time. In talking about the Kessel trade, Cullen recalled how it was perceived. This wasn't a slam dunk. Kessel didn't have the best reputation around the league, especially among coaches who would get frustrated with his lack of training dedication at times. There was a healthy and very public debate by the Penguins management team at the end of day two on the draft floor in Florida about whether or not to do the Kessel deal. It's easy to forget all that now.

"That was a really risky move at the time," Cullen said. "That's swinging for the fences. It could go wrong. You already have a lot of stars on your team. You don't fully know. Clearly he had done a lot of homework on it and knew the person behind the player. That's one of his strengths is his ability to evaluate a player behind the scenes and get an understanding of how it works. You can argue we don't win a Stanley Cup or two without Phil. No question. He was as good as anyone in that playoff run. That's one thing I always admired about Jim, he was not afraid to take chances."

It's less of a risk when you know exactly what your team needs. When you have the pulse of the organization. Cullen noticed the same thing Sullivan did. Cullen would go to meetings and Rutherford usually wasn't the one doing the talking. He was sitting back and listening.

"It was interesting to me how innovative and open to ideas he was. You saw how he adapted to the game changing. He was open to listening and humble enough to know he didn't know everything," Cullen said. "He valued the opinions of the people around him. That always hit me, watching him work as a Hall of Fame GM. He acted with so much humility in that way."

In 2016, the Penguins won their first Stanley Cup since 2009.

A team that seemed destined to win a bunch of them after Sidney Crosby and Evgeni Malkin beat the Red Wings for their first Cup in 2009 had finally gotten back on top. They did it behind decisive moves—firing coach Mike Johnston and replacing him with Mike Sullivan. Trading for Phil Kessel. Trading for Carl Hagelin. Trading for Trevor Daley. These weren't the moves of a general manager shooting from the hip, as Rutherford has been accused of doing. These were the moves of someone who knew exactly what his team needed. And when.

It was close to midnight after the Penguins won that Cup against the Sharks and Rutherford was back in his San Jose hotel room with his family getting ready to celebrate with the rest of the team. His son, James, enjoying the high of the moment, said, "Dad, let's do that again."

Rutherford leaned back comfortably in his chair.

"We're going to do it again next year," he said.

It was out of character for someone both humble and also aware that you don't push the hockey gods too far. But he felt it. His wife, Leslie, and daughter, Andrea, looked at each other with tears in their eyes. It was an incredible moment in time for a family that had been through every step of the process with Rutherford. In 2017, the Penguins beat the Nashville Predators in the Stanley Cup Final to cement the Crosby Penguins as one of the rare dynasty teams of the salary cap era. When it looked like the Chicago Blackhawks or Los Angeles Kings might dominate the discussion, the combination of Crosby, Malkin, and Rutherford was the right one in the right time.

Sullivan doesn't remember which of those Cups it was after, but shortly after winning one of them, he found himself back in a restaurant with Jim Rutherford, as they had been so many times before on the road. This time, it was a place called Bruneaux in Sewickley, Pennsylvania. This time, the entire coaching and hockey operations staff was there, with their families. This time, they were joined by the Stanley Cup. The outdoor patio was sectioned off, with a fire going on the huge outdoor stone fireplace, wood stacked on either side. Cigars were smoked as everyone relaxed on the outdoor patio furniture. Eventually, they enjoyed a nice meal, French cuisine, from a menu that featured everything from vegetable Napoleon to bouillabaisse.

At one point, Rutherford and Sullivan found themselves next to the Cup. They leaned in, touching it with pride—this one was all theirs—and took a picture. Sullivan would later hang that picture in his living room. It's a reminder of what happens when someone takes the time to listen—*really listen*—in order to build trust and, when it's time, act.

It was late November in 2021 and Francesco Aquilini was at the front door of the Rutherfords' North Carolina home. When Jim Rutherford told his wife, Leslie, that the owner of the Vancouver Canucks was going to travel across the continent to their home, she thought a couple of things. One, this has never happened to them before. And two, this is a man who cares deeply about making the right hire.

"He obviously loves this team, cares about his team, and is passionate about his team," Leslie said.

What do you do when a billionaire is swinging by on a recruiting mission? Make sandwiches? Order a pizza? Leslie settled on putting together a large charcuterie board so Aquilini and her husband could pick at a few cured meats and sliced cheeses while they talked hockey and the future of the Vancouver Canucks. Aquilini presented his vision for the team. He explained his version of events that had happened over the years with the Canucks. He told Rutherford where he wanted his franchise going in the coming years. As the hours-long conversation continued, Rutherford's uncertainty as to whether or not he was going to return to the game in an official capacity started slipping away.

"That was pretty special," Rutherford said.

After Aquilini left, Jim and Leslie talked things over. She never believed he was going to retire anyway, and this looked like a real opportunity to work for someone who cared about winning, even if he hadn't always gone about it the right way in the past.

"If you're in, I'm in," she told Jim.

A few months earlier, when Rutherford and I were sitting outside the first tee of that Pittsburgh country club, I tried to distill down decades' worth of team building and leadership to one thing. Rutherford, at that point, had done it all. He was in the Hall. He had three Cup rings. If anyone had the answer, it was him.

So what was the most important job of an NHL general manager?

There was no hesitation.

"Managing up," he answered.

Managing up. Managing ownership. The answer every general manager might think, but the one they rarely give.

"Everybody is afraid to say it," Rutherford said. "There's nothing wrong with saying it. There's nothing wrong with saying you need to manage the person you report to and the people above them. You need to communicate with them, you need to explain to them what you're thinking and what you're doing. There's absolutely nothing wrong with that."

Rutherford was so convicted both in his belief that it's the most important thing and that it's okay to say it out loud that he repeated it the following December. On a dais. Next to his new boss. In front of a room full of media. During his introduction to the Vancouver market, with Aquilini by his side, Rutherford shared his opinion that managing up was the most important part of being an NHL GM. In writing about the moment, *The Athletic*'s Thomas Drance put it this way: "It was a brilliant formulation, in part because of its simplicity. In the presence of Aquilini, Rutherford at once addressed the elephant in the room and made the topic seem miniature."

The autonomy of management in Vancouver had been in question for years under Aquilini. And here you had a new team president acknowledging, in the most public way, that it was going to be crucial for him to manage the guy immediately to his right to succeed in running the Canucks. As we discussed this theory of management, Rutherford said it so casually that he made it sound almost simple.

It isn't.

"It's not just in hockey or in sports. It's in life," he said. "As a kid, how do you manage your parents? How do you manage your teacher in school? This is something we naturally do all the way through our life, but nobody wants to admit it."

Rutherford is good at it. It started with a big personality in Karmanos. It continued under Ron Burkle and Mario Lemieux. Now Aquilini. Each of those owners had become successful in a different way. Each had personality traits that made them wildly successful in business and in hockey. And each had to be handled differently, but with a common through line from Ruther-ford.

"Just be honest. Tell them how you feel. Let them have their voice, which they obviously deserve," Rutherford said. "And try to talk through it. And if you can't talk through it, you'll have a problem at some point. But for the most points in my career, I never had a problem."

Karmanos, for instance, has a strong personality. When he would take a position on something, he wasn't budging in the moment. So Rutherford learned to listen. He heard Karmanos out and then let it settle. If he still disagreed a couple of days later, he'd circle back and try again. "Don't lock horns that first time you're talking about an issue you don't agree on," Rutherford said. "Just let it sit. Then go back and see if there's an appropriate time you can revisit that situation. And he always opened the door to it, he never ever shut that down."

Some people who worked for Karmanos once had a police sketch artist draw a picture of him as a gift with the caption: *Ready. Fire. Aim.* That's how he operated.

"Jimmy was good at slowing him down," Craig said. "For me, it's such a positive. You're dealing with someone who has built their own business, run their own business, and in most cases managed their own business. Most of these owners are somebody who bring somebody in to run the hockey team for them. . . . In Pete, you've got a guy that, the first time he ever gave up control of anything was to Jim Rutherford to run the hockey team."

The payoff for these owners was hockey immortality. They got their names etched in silver. They put their trust in a guy they believed was honest, who they knew was hardworking, was bold when he needed to be bold, but maybe more importantly, sat and listened when he needed to listen. There's a humility in that. It's a defining trait of the man who helped Carolina's first owner win a Stanley Cup. And humility is probably not the first word used to describe Carolina's next owner, something I discovered up close after flying to Long Island to spend time with him during a Hurricanes playoff game.

CHAPTER 7

BETTER, FASTER, CHEAPER

I'm coming in and trying to acquire new information and debate it, and that might be unconventional . . . but there's a difference between unconventional and wrong.

—**Tom Dundon**

It was a unique setting for an NHL team during the Stanley Cup playoffs. The Carolina Hurricanes were staying at a Long Island Hyatt about twenty minutes or so from UBS Arena, home of their playoff series opponent, the New York Islanders. As you pull up to this hotel from the airport, the first thing you see is the massive horse track. The whole place is huge—restaurants, casino, and hotel in a giant complex. Go through the double doors, over to the Starbucks near the check-in desk, and it's a mix of airline employees who want to stay near the airport, gamblers in between pulls on the slot machines, and, when I arrived, Hurricanes center Paul Stastny in flip-flops grabbing a venti coffee to start the day.

My room wasn't ready, so I joined Stastny in ordering a coffee then set up shop with my laptop and headphones in the lobby. I looked forward to the conversation with Carolina Hurricanes owner Tom Dundon, but also appreciated the extra time to make sure I didn't miss any recent business deals. His path to Hurricanes ownership was a bit thin on public details that skim along from failed restaurateur to subprime loans to billionaire. He was an early investor in Topgolf and bought an entire pickleball league. On the day we met, there was also a lawsuit pending for his involvement in the Alliance of American Football. It was hard to figure what to make of him, which made me a bit uneasy. He stands out. See him at a league event or on the draft floor and he always looks the same, wearing a tracksuit and hat, surrounded by colleagues in suits and ties. While waiting to chat with him, I sent a quick text to someone who once worked for him to get a better sense of what he's like.

"That's a loaded question," came the reply.

Not exactly reassuring. I'd learn that he's a guy who believes he can fix just about anything in business, and I was reading about his attempt to buy the rental car company Hertz when he walked into the hotel lobby with Don Waddell, then the Hurricanes GM and president.

I've known Waddell forever. He was the GM of the Atlanta Thrashers when I first started writing about hockey in 2007. That first spring was fun, with Waddell's Thrashers reaching the playoffs for the first time in franchise history. But the success didn't last. The team was swept in the first round and the following season it got bad enough that Waddell also had to step in as the coach. Before long, we were all gone. I moved home to Detroit. Waddell ended up in Carolina. And the Thrashers in Winnipeg.

But our long history makes for easy conversation. He wondered what I was doing hanging out in the Hurricanes' team hotel. I explained that I wanted to learn how Tom Dundon operated. And his unspoken reaction, the raised eyebrows, suggested I might be in for more than I was anticipating.

Dundon offered up a water and we looked for a quiet place to chat. I wanted to avoid the lobby, where players were constantly passing through, like defenseman Brent Burns waiting a few feet away outside the bank of elevators. So we walked down a hallway to the team meeting room, where the players had eaten breakfast earlier in the morning. The trainers were wrapping up a meeting across the room and Dundon spoke quietly while they were there. As soon as the room emptied, the atmosphere shifted.

"Ask me about whatever you want," Dundon said.

So much of what seems to separate how Tom Dundon operates is centered on value. How he values an employee. How he values a player. How he values a decision. How he values an offer sheet. How he values a broadcaster. His path to NHL owner started with how he valued a hockey franchise.

There might not be another person in hockey who adheres to these values as strictly as Dundon. When he gets the biggest blowback publicly or even internally, it's because of a difference in perception of value.

Jason Kulas has known Dundon since his days at Southern Methodist University. In the business world, Kulas has witnessed, and benefited, from Dundon's relentless ability to assess value, work tirelessly to find ways to improve value, and find opportunities to create even more. For ten years, Kulas said, he talked every single day with Dundon about building the subprime auto finance company Santander Consumer USA. Subprime lenders give loans to borrowers with poor credit who wouldn't normally get approved for a loan, usually at much higher interest rates.

In January 2007, when Dundon's founding partners decided to cash out, Kulas left J.P. Morgan to join Dundon as the company's CFO. According to Kulas, Dundon opted not to cash out, but to roll his equity back into purchasing the company in a bet on himself that he could keep it growing. During the financial crisis that hit the world during that time, they saw opportunity and made $36 billion of acquisitions. Over the next ten years, Kulas said they took the company from $4 billion in managed assets to $54 billion. If you're cool with the concept of subprime lending, it's undeniably impressive growth.

Dundon did it by diving into the details. If one of his employees started in on a story on why something was valuable, he'd counter that if he wanted a story, he'd buy a book. He wanted data. He was relentless in his pursuit of information and questioning how decisions were made. This would be an important mindset when it came to how he'd approach and sometimes clash with hockey establishment.

"He processes information by talking things through with many different people," Kulas said. "He's got those earbuds around his neck—he's constantly on the phone working through different angles of an issue."

Constant. It's the best word to describe Dundon. His focus is constantly trying to make things better, faster, and cheaper. It means calls at all hours. It can grind down the kind of people who might not respond to that kind of pressure, who might be turned off by a billionaire who can't turn off the obsession with saving money. But he tends to find and promote people who respond to that pressure, and it has worked for him.

"Here's the thing. People follow Tom because he's a winner," Kulas said. "Even if it is challenging and hectic because he's always pushing for better, faster, cheaper. It never lets up. But people want to be on a winning team, they'll go through all that because of the result."

According to Auto Finance News, Dundon left Santander in 2015 during heightened regulatory pressure on the company, and in 2017 the two sides ultimately agreed on an exit deal that paid Dundon $942 million for his stock and $66 million in severance. His relentless pursuit of better, faster, and cheaper made him a billionaire. It also allowed him to enter the rarified space of professional sports ownership.

When Dundon first decided to buy a team, he thought it might be in the NBA or in football. He looked hard at a couple of basketball teams, including the Houston Rockets. He considered buying a piece of the Dallas Mavericks from Mark Cuban. What he appreciated about Cuban is that he bought the team and poured so much attention into the fan experience. Dundon doesn't come from money, so he knows what it's like to try to buy a five-dollar ticket or sneak into a game for nothing. And he appreciated that the Mavericks seemed to be giving people value for the cost of attending their games, something that wasn't the case before Cuban.

"When he bought the Mavericks, you wouldn't have been proud to own the Mavericks," Dundon said. "They made it fun."

It was a strategy he'd tuck away for when he ever got a team. That opportunity presented itself when a banker from Allen &

Company, a New York–based investment firm known for broker-ing professional sports transactions, called him.

If you want to buy a team, we have one you can buy right now.

Dundon isn't necessarily a hockey guy. He grew up watch-ing hockey. He was nine years old when the Miracle on Ice happened, a memorable moment for every American sports fan coming of age in 1980. He didn't play hockey, but when the Stars moved from Minnesota to Dallas, he went to as many games as he could. That's the extent of his hockey background. When the banker called and said he could buy the Carolina Hurricanes, his lack of hockey background and knowledge didn't slow him down. At this point, you could argue it's been an advantage.

"My belief, right or wrong, is—it ain't that hard," Dundon said. "All the people around me—the players know, the coaches know, the scouts know—I have enough subject matter experts. There's plenty of subject matter experts. What I'd like to think—to the extent that what I do helps, since not all of it does—there is something that has happened in my experiences that, added to their experiences, hopefully is accretive."

When he got the call from Allen & Company, his frustration around not being able to land a team was growing, so he decided to check it out. For someone who made a lot of money uncovering opportunity, what he saw on the Hurricanes' balance sheet was the opposite. According to a *Forbes* story written at the time of the sale from Peter Karmanos Jr. to Dundon, the team had $100 million in debt. They hadn't made the playoffs since 2009, a nine-season stretch. Their average attendance in 2016–17 had dropped to under twelve thousand fans per game. There wasn't a ton to like, even if he *was* a die-hard hockey fan. Dundon's conclusion when he saw the numbers: "It's not investable. I went there and I went to a preseason game. There's nobody there. . . . I didn't think the math worked."

He bought it anyway. For once, when the math didn't make sense, he invested.

"I just decided I'd make a noneconomic decision and do it because it looked like fun," he said.

In January 2018, he bought 52 percent of the team, according to the Associated Press. In 2021, he became the sole owner of the Hurricanes after buying out the remaining shares from Karmanos. Even if he bought the team for fun, bought because it was something he'd always wanted to do, bought, by his own admission, for his ego, there was still a thought process to it all. He estimated that if he purchased the team, he'd win a Stanley Cup about 3 percent of the time. If he did an average job as owner, he'd make the playoffs 50 percent of the time. If he was above average he might be able to push that to 60 percent of the time.

He tried to get answers from people in the organization about how supportive Raleigh would be if they consistently made the playoffs. He knew Raleigh was a great place to live and he knew there were great fans. He also knew it didn't have a great corporate base, and without consumer brands, he couldn't count on Fortune 500 companies spending on the team.

"There was a set of challenges in the market," he said. "People don't grow up thinking about hockey. It's different than it is in the more traditional markets. To say it's a nontraditional market, people take it as an insult. It's just reality."

So like he did in pouring his equity back into his auto finance company, Dundon made another bet. If the market would support a consistently successful team, he thought he could make it work because he was confident he could operate it at an above-average success rate.

"I always felt, knowing nothing, I'm going to be at the top end of whatever it is. There was no doubt in my mind. I never think I'm not going to win. I always think we'll figure it out. Hire the right people and we'll figure it out," he said.

And so the obsession became on building sustainable success. For this to work in Raleigh, this couldn't be a team of fits and starts. This couldn't be a team that might go on a long playoff run one year and miss the playoffs for the next five. The thought of pushing in for short-term success couldn't regularly be part of the equation. Everything became about managing today and tomorrow at the same exact time.

"It's a different incentive structure," he said. "We're still going to play hockey next year. . . . It's easy for fans and everything to get into 'What are we eating today?' I worry more about what am I going to eat tomorrow."

It would be about sustainability. Every decision would be made through that lens.

"It's all I care about. I don't think you can move your odds that much [with short-term moves]. I can prove it. I know the market disagrees with me. Full stop. They disagree with me. That you should do things for short-term gain," he said. "I'm saying, I don't even know when you do those things you really can change. You don't change your outcome very much. When you win, people look back and say how smart [the short-term move] was. When you lose, no one remembers. No one remembers the other teams."

This would be his approach. This is how he'd run the Carolina Hurricanes. A constant obsession with improvement.

Constant calls to gather opinions from everyone in the organization. Demands for data, not tradition.

Better, faster, cheaper. Better, faster, cheaper. Better, faster, cheaper.

The first time Carolina Hurricanes assistant GM Eric Tulsky met Dundon, he had no idea who he was. He was introduced to him by former Hurricanes GM Ron Francis during a preseason game before the 2017–18 regular season. He wasn't introduced as a prospective new owner or the guy who could determine Tulsky's NHL career path.

"I assumed it was a sponsor or a friend," Tulsky said.

It made the barrage of questions puzzling. In 2015, the Carolina Hurricanes hired Tulsky full-time as a hockey analyst. Tulsky, who has a BA in chemistry and physics from Harvard and a PhD in chemistry from UC Berkeley, had been sharing his hockey analytics writing on an SB Nation blog while working in nanotechnology. The joke in Carolina is that it took Dundon meeting Tulsky to finally concede he wasn't the smartest guy in the room.

On the night of this preseason game, Tulsky was introduced as the manager of analytics for the team, so Dundon's questions were primarily analytically driven. At one point, a player attempted to pass the puck across the slot to a player on the back door of the crease and the pass was broken up. Dundon immediately wanted to know the odds. Should he have shot? How often does that shot go in? Was the pass the better move? How often does that pass connect, and when it does how often is there a goal?

He got answers and then started pushing back. He challenged any assumptions being made.

"He went a hundred miles per hour, just a constant stream of questions," Tulsky said. "'Why'd this player do this? Why'd this player do that? What's your expected goal model say?' I don't know who this guy is, I'm not going to tell him that. It was a whirlwind."

It made an impression. And what Tulsky learned quickly when Dundon bought the team was that was how he operated all the time. The first impression would be the lasting impression because he'd see it every day. His cell phone call log is loaded with incoming calls from the owner.

"Probably more than anyone else I've ever met, he looks for ways to improve everything you do and everything about everything you do," Tulsky said. "And so that started from day one. He wanted to meet with each person, hear about everything they did and question every aspect of it and try to find the places where there was room for improvement."

For Tulsky, that approach wasn't going to be a problem. Now that Dundon owned the team, if he wanted to see the data, he could see the data. And Tulsky had only been with an NHL organization a couple of years, so he didn't have decades of ingrained beliefs in how a hockey team should be run. When Dundon bought the team, he was told to hire a general manager and coach, give them three years, and if they didn't win, fire them, find a replacement, and start over again. That strategy didn't make sense to Dundon. He wanted to dive in and learn everything about the organization so that if something went wrong, it was on him, not the person he hired. The first part of doing that is to challenge the way everything is done in the organization. Especially since he was buying a team that hadn't made the playoffs in nearly a decade and was losing money. Even the most skeptical person in the organization had to realize that the status quo probably wasn't the best path forward.

That's what Dundon did. He started questioning everything.

"In any business, that's what anybody does. I think I could take over almost any company and make it better. In my mind, I think that. I don't know if that's right. But you couldn't convince me it's not. The only way to do that, to make it better, is to find out what's not right," he said. "If you look at where the Hurricanes were, the idea that they didn't need to question everything—it doesn't make any sense."

Hindsight makes that sound completely reasonable. The Hurricanes' lack of success before Dundon makes it sound reasonable. Often that's the way with Dundon. He explains things so logically and matter-of-factly that it's easy to just nod and accept the thought process. But the person running the organization when Dundon joined was Ron Francis. Francis is one of the most respected people in hockey. He won two Stanley Cups as a player, and when he retired, only Wayne Gretzky had more career assists. He joined the Hurricanes front office and eventually worked his way up to the general manager position in 2014. It didn't take Dundon long to realize his approach—the constant questioning of everything—wasn't going to work with Francis.

"It wasn't that I came in and tried to sabotage him or tried to fire him. It was 'I'm going to ask every question why is it this way and I start from a position of 'This is bad,'" Dundon said. "People don't like to be told 'This is bad.'"

"Hockey people don't like that," Dundon continued. "I've looked at other companies and done other things—no one likes it.

It ain't just hockey. They don't like it when you come in and say, 'This isn't good enough. We're going to do it better. We're going to do it my way, but my way means everyone gets a say, not just the boss.' When I go talk to the trainers and the players and the scouts and the fans and the NHL and other teams and reporters, I talk to everybody. I'm on the phone ten hours a day—agents, everybody. I'm gathering information. If you've been doing this your whole life, you're not. You're just not. You have the information you've acquired. I'm coming in and trying to acquire new information and debate it, and that might be unconventional. That might be unconventional, but there's a difference between unconventional and wrong."

In 2018, Dundon reassigned Francis to another position in the front office and decided to embark on a search for a new general manager. A month later, the team announced in a three-sentence press release that they had terminated Francis's contract. Firing Francis certainly got the NHL's attention. So did the hunt for a general manager. Dundon had conversations with the candidates who were viewed as up-and-coming executives at the time, guys like Paul Fenton, Mike Futa, Steve Greeley, and Tom Fitzgerald. But during a high-profile *Hockey Night in Canada* segment where these names were being reported, Nick Kypreos reported that Dundon was only offering candidates around $400,000 to run the team. That person would also have to report to Dundon. So the first impression he made on those around the league was firing a highly respected Hall of Famer. His second was refusing to pay the going rate for his replacement.

"The philosophy was 'Can you show me anything that says some GM is better than the market over time?' I don't think the Carolina Hurricanes could figure out how to gain an advantage in that spot," Dundon said, confirming that he didn't want to pay the typical rate for a GM. "My thought was, I would take somebody less experienced but that I liked and was smart and we'd all work together with Roddy [Brind'Amour], and I was going to keep Don [Waddell] around. My deal was, Don was a GM for a long time, he's here, I like him. I already have someone here. I know that I'm going to be able to take the information, work with people and, I believe, gain some advantage in some areas. The idea—I had just gone through what I'd gone through with Francis. The last thing I wanted was to bring someone in who didn't want to be part of the way I ran things."

And so he didn't make the hire. Don Waddell added general manager duties to his duties as team president in May 2018 and the search for a new addition to the front office was over. A couple of months later, another high-profile decision helped feed a growing perception that Dundon might not be as wealthy as other owners. After thirty-eight years as a broadcaster, Hall of Fame radio voice Chuck Kaiton declined a substantial pay cut and walked away from the Carolina Hurricanes as their play-by-play voice. Dundon offered him the ability to make up for the gap in pay by selling radio sponsorships, which is typically something asked at the lower levels of broadcasters. For instance, Kaiton did it when he was doing radio for the University of Wisconsin in the 1970s while earning $100 per game and chasing his dream.

In explaining these decisions early in his tenure, Dundon is careful to do it in a way that is respectful to what Francis and Kaiton bring to an NHL franchise. He believes Francis is a smart executive, just not someone who works well with his methods. He believes Kaiton is a great radio voice, just not someone who it makes sense for the Carolina Hurricanes to pay a premium to employ. In his mind, offering to put $100,000 toward having Kaiton on the radio and giving him the ad inventory was a charitable act since, in his mind, this was an area of the ledger sheet that should cost him nothing, with the ability to simulcast the television broadcast.

To Kaiton, it was a huge pay cut and an insult.

If you're relentless about finding ways to make the companies you run better, faster, and cheaper, these decisions can be easily justified. It's impossible, after all, to measure the value of one fan who hears Kaiton call a game at night on the radio, closes their eyes, imagines Jordan Staal scoring that overtime goal, and falls in love with hockey. In 1979, Kaiton was hired to call games for the Hartford Whalers. He did that for nearly twenty years before following the Whalers to Carolina, where he continued calling games for the franchise. He's been out of Hartford since the late 1990s and yet, every year the Minor League Baseball franchise in Hartford, the Yard Goats, bring him back as part of their Whalers Alumni Weekend. Fans line up for hours to get autographs of former Whalers as well as from Kaiton. They share stories of listening to the games, of how much they miss the team, and those late nights with the radio on.

"It's an overwhelming response," Kaiton said. "I'm one of the people who signs autographs. It's amazing how much time they want to spend with you. I have a lot of time. We stay for the game. We talk with fans. You have to have time for people, that's what it's all about."

The same thing happens when he runs into Hurricanes fans in Raleigh. There's an organizational cost when someone like Kaiton leaves, but it's not easy to calculate. Others have also exited the organization, told that if they wanted to make more money it would have to be with a different franchise.

It's always about a difference in value.

"I just wish there'd be a side of his philosophy that values the intangibles," Kaiton said. "That's the best way to put it. People bring a lot of different things to the table in that organization. I don't know if he appreciates them or not. . . . You wish he would appreciate the people who work for him."

Tough decisions are made. Reputations are built. And the belief around hockey outside Carolina started to build in his early years that Dundon was cheap. That he might not even be able to afford the kinds of signing bonuses star players demand. It's not a huge leap to make that conclusion if he's letting a radio guy go over a couple of hundred thousand dollars.

For anyone making that assumption, it ended up being a big miscalculation.

———

On the morning of July 1, 2019, a couple hours before the start of free agency, the Carolina Hurricanes received a phone call from the Montreal Canadiens. The Habs were planning on signing Hurricanes star Sebastian Aho to an offer sheet. Contract talks between Aho and the Hurricanes weren't progressing and the fastest way to get a deal done is to find one elsewhere if you're a restricted free agent. Aho did exactly that.

"When we heard there was an offer sheet coming in, we were worried it would be an amount genuinely difficult to match," Tulsky said. "Because that's what you worry about when you hear there's an offer sheet."

Aho and the Canadiens had agreed on a five-year deal worth $8.454 million per season. If the Hurricanes chose not to match the deal, they'd receive a first-, second-, and third-round draft pick. In a league that is generally conservative in its utilization of an offer sheet—the last one before Aho was six years earlier when Ryan O'Reilly signed with the Calgary Flames—this deal was an aberration. The reason general managers typically don't use offer sheets as a tool to acquire players is fairly simple: they don't believe it works. Teams usually match the offer and now all you've done is anger an opposing franchise. You've given another franchise a reason to try and mess up your salary structure and go after your own young players.

One of my favorite conversations ever about this topic was with former Kings GM Dean Lombardi when he was assembling what would end up being a multi-Cup-winning roster. When I asked if he was concerned about rival teams signing his young players to offer sheets, he came out firing.

"We're not only going to match any offer sheet, we'll have enough space to go after your guys. Go ahead and make our day. If you sign our guy, we're coming back with both barrels firing. You'd better be damn straight that you have the cap space and all your guys are signed," Lombardi answered.

So yeah, you'd better be sure you know what you're doing if you go this route.

The Canadiens had reason to believe this one might work. At least based on what was publicly known about Carolina's new owner. He'd cut ties with a popular radio voice over money. He wasn't willing to pay the top general manager candidates what was generally the accepted rate to have someone run the organization. There also wasn't a ton of public information about Dundon available. When he was at Santander, he didn't see a lot of value in being a public-facing executive, so he kept a low profile. There was definitely a question about how he was willing to spend money and if the Hurricanes were even doing well enough financially to match an offer sheet. There was also the belief that Dundon might take a principled stand against player signing bonuses, which was another part of the strategy.

When the Hurricanes saw the structure of the deal, they discovered it was heavy in signing bonuses, containing the maximum amount. Aho would get the minimum salary, the rest in bonuses and, as NHL insider Chris Johnston shared on the day of the signing, he'd be owed more than $21 million in just the first calendar year. It's exactly how you'd structure a deal if either you thought that Dundon didn't have the money or had a moral stance against massive signing bonuses.

"The perception was different than reality," Dundon said. "That only happened because they perceived—I don't know if they thought I didn't have the money or I was too stubborn. But I'm not stubborn. I'm practical."

Once he saw the offer from Montreal, it took seconds to conclude he'd match it. The strategy falls apart pretty quickly if paying the actual salary isn't an issue. Seeing the actual deal ended up being a relief for those in the Hurricanes front office. The only decision they were struggling with was whether they'd leave the Canadiens hanging for a week or if they'd match immediately to send a message to their fans.

"I just want us to win and I want to protect the [salary cap]," Dundon said. "I've got money for generations. This is stupid. But I have a right and wrong way to do things. I still turn the lights off when I leave the room. I still set the air conditioners properly. I still teach my kids you can't just order food on Uber. . . . It doesn't mean I don't have money, it means I respect it and there's a fiduciary duty to not be ridiculous."

Two years later, the Hurricanes went Dean Lombardi on the Canadiens. Now, Dundon says revenge wasn't the intention. He said that in the summer of 2021, they tried to use their cap space elsewhere in an attempt to improve their roster. It just turns out that the Montreal Canadiens had an unsigned restricted free agent on their roster in twenty-one-year-old center Jesperi Kotkaniemi, who was the third-overall pick in the 2018 draft, and also a top-three talent on the Hurricanes' internal draft list. Organizationally, the team believes strongly in building down the middle, and their underlying analytics suggested that Kotkaniemi had a high floor as a young center. They also noticed Montreal was up against the cap. They believed they could structure a deal in a way that made it hard for the Canadiens to match.

"I don't know if they hadn't done it to us if we would have done it," Dundon said. "But I can assure you, we wouldn't do it if we didn't think it was a good idea. I would be stupid to think—why would I lower my chance of winning?"

Dundon said that they didn't want to do this publicly. He said, once they decided that Kotkaniemi was a target, their preference was to make a trade.

"More than anything, offer sheets aren't how you build your team," he said. "There's more other efficient ways. When you look at the compensation plus what you have to pay, it's almost impossible for that to be a good strategy. And most players don't want to leave."

The Hurricanes called the Canadiens and said they were going to sign Kotkaniemi to an offer sheet. They let them know the terms of the deal. They let them know they preferred to make a trade that would have potentially given the Canadiens a better return than they would get from the offer sheet, a first- and third-round pick. Montreal was interested in Seth Jarvis, which was a nonstarter for the Hurricanes.

The two sides couldn't agree on a trade, so the Hurricanes went all in.

They made the offer—a one-year deal worth $6.1 million. Then they announced it on Twitter. In French. They also tweeted an Uno reverse card that further fueled the belief that this was retribution. They changed their Twitter bio from English to French. They added a $20 signing bonus, which happens to be Sebastian Aho's number. The social media barrage sure made it hard to suggest that revenge wasn't a factor.

"I called the [social media] guy and said enough," Dundon said. Dundon also heard from the NHL about the public shots at the Canadiens.

"I got a call saying, 'What's the endgame here?' I'm like, 'No, we're done. It's over,'" Dundon said. "I wish they had come back at us. That would have been good for the league. That would be funny. When they didn't . . . there's a point we went too far."

A week later it became official: the Canadiens declined to match the Hurricanes offer and for only the second time in the salary cap era, a team executed a successful offer sheet. Less than a year later, Carolina would lock Kotkaniemi in on an eight-year deal worth $4.82 million per season.

By the time that contract extension was done, there weren't many people in hockey saying that Dundon wasn't willing to spend on players. If there's value, he'll do it, and Dundon made a bet that a highly skilled young center would outperform that contract over the life of the deal.

"His relentless desire to improve and lack of concern about what people will say if it doesn't work out means we've probably taken more risks than other teams do," Tulsky said. "We've been more comfortable saying, 'If this deal doesn't work, we'll do another one.' I think that comes back to his philosophy that there are always ways to improve."

———————

Throughout our conversation in the hotel conference room converted into a Hurricanes team meal hub, an occasional player would stroll in to grab a drink or a snack. They'd spot Dundon, come over and stay for a quick chat. Sometimes he'd ask if they were headed to the horse track on their open Saturday afternoon.

"You going to go over there? You going to gamble?" Dundon asked as a player stopped to chat.

"Maybe ten bucks."

"Because you're smart."

"I've never seen a horse race before, what else am I going to do?"

"Yeah, you've got to go."

As the players left, you could already see the wheels turning. Defenseman Brett Pesce dropped by for a quick chat, and as he walked away Dundon lamented a tough decision he'd have to face down the road with one of his best players. Pesce had one year left on his contract and his price tag was going to go up considerably, and he was entering his thirties. For a guy desperate for sustained success, you could see he was already grappling with where it might be headed.

But the lengthiest conversation—by a long shot—was with

a kid I didn't recognize. Mackenzie MacEachern had just been called up from the AHL after scoring eleven goals in thirty-seven games for the Chicago Wolves. MacEachern thought initially it was to be a member of the black aces, the playoff practice squad, but that would change quickly. There were injuries to the Hurricanes forwards that cut deep during this playoff run. Enough that Dundon, in this moment, was telling MacEachern to expect to play the next day.

Dundon then started grilling him about the players in Chicago. He wanted to know everything. How was Ryan Suzuki doing? How much muscle did MacEachern think he put on? Was a different teammate still unwilling to go to the tough areas? Who had the best shot of playing consistently in the NHL? Did he think goalie Pyotr Kochetkov could play in the NHL?

MacEachern walked a balance between providing information for the owner of his team and staying positive about teammates he had just been playing with in the minors. He had nothing but positive answers for Dundon, who pushed back just enough to show that he knew each of these players well, including their deficiencies.

This conversation wouldn't have surprised Carolina assistant GM Darren Yorke. He's been on the receiving end of many Friday night calls while watching the AHL team play, when Dundon would call to ask about a specific player or coaching strategies in that game.

"To be that dedicated then forces everyone in the organization to raise the bar," Yorke said.

Sports are filled with rich owners who have had success in building their core business only to fail miserably by being too hands-on in how they ran their sports franchise. Generally, the best strategy is to hire somebody you trust who is an expert in that space and let them do their job. If the Hurricanes win a Stanley Cup, Dundon will be the exception. That they're in the mix every year might already qualify him for that status. If he's successful, it's because he's not parachuting in to make the big decisions. He's in on the details every single day.

"What people don't know—they think he's this owner who has his hand in everything, like it's a negative. You get a negative overtone. It's the opposite," said his coach, Rod Brind'Amour. "Name an owner in sports who knows every minor leaguer on the team. And makes sure it's a good fit. And watches the minor-league games. Forget about our games, he's watching those. It's pretty impressive for a guy who didn't know about hockey. He's teaching himself and comes to us with phone calls. What happened here? Why did we do that? He wants to learn. He tests you all the time."

Yorke thinks the AHL example might explain Dundon's success best. On the day we're chatting, the neighbor Carolina Panthers had just fired coach Frank Reich. Owner David Tepper, who had only been in the NFL owners club five years, had just named his seventh head coach. It wasn't going well for Carolina's NFL cousins.

"If you're involved, but you're not involved in terms of gathering information, but you just want to make decisions, regardless of what business you're in, it's not going to go well," Yorke said.

Dundon demands the information. He demands the explanation on every decision—big or small—made by the people on his staff. It's all completely rational, almost so rational that emotion has been removed.

Until game day.

It was Sunday afternoon and Game 4 of a first-round playoff series between the Hurricanes and the Islanders was about to begin. Dundon entered his suite for the afternoon wearing his uniform—black track pants, black hoodie, and a black Hurricanes hat. In a league with a deep culture of respecting the game by dressing in a certain way, this decision makes him an outsider. His team was playing a franchise run by Lou Lamoriello, and even without getting a visual that afternoon, it's safe to say Lamoriello wasn't in track pants. It was a loud, standing-room-only crowd in UBS Arena, and the way the suites are set up, Dundon was surrounded by Islanders fans. The suite to the left was jammed, friends and families in Islanders jerseys rooting against the team owned by the man on their right. Dundon was joined by a couple of friends, who took in the game by Dundon's side, leaning in on a countertop overlooking three rows of empty foldout leather chairs in the owner's suite. The room behind him had a flat-screen television that he'd occasionally watch for replays.

At one point, Carolina forward Jack Drury was cross-checked into the boards by Ryan Pulock and was in pain, his hands on his head and his legs kicking. It was the first time Dundon left his spot overlooking the action. He walked over to an island in the middle of the suite to watch the replay.

"You can't do that," he said. In this moment, he was like any other Hurricane fan assuming this hit on Drury would be a major penalty because Drury appeared to be concussed as he left the ice. After a lengthy delay, an announcement was made. The call had been downgraded to a minor, and Dundon was livid.

"If he has a little cut and there's blood, it's four," he said to one of his friends. "But he has a concussion and it's two."

"He's out for the game," his friend said, agreeing with Dundon's conclusion that the call was too light.

"He'll be out for the series," Dundon predicted.

The Islanders came out extremely aggressively in this game. They were physical. They started fights, and in the moment, Dundon was concerned. He didn't like the scrums after the whistles or the hits into the board.

"It's not good for us when this shit starts," he said. "We don't do this shit."

The owner who was driven by data, values, and logic was replaced by someone experiencing the emotions of a hockey game like anyone else. For someone who believes he's always going to figure out a way to win, the randomness that comes with a sport like hockey can be frustrating.

"If we lose a game, he wants to sell the team," said Rod Brind'Amour. "He's so invested. He hates losing."

"I hate it," Dundon said. "The only way I'll sell it is if somebody gets me right after we lose."

Despite his early frustrations, there would be no selling of the team following this game. The Hurricanes would take advantage of bad penalties by the Islanders with a couple of power play goals that would hold up. And it was the AHL call-up who Dundon chatted with making the biggest impact. Before grilling Mackenzie MacEachern on every player on the Hurricanes' AHL roster the day before, Dundon gave him a bit of advice.

If you get a shot, take it.

MacEachern's third-period goal against the Islanders, his first career playoff goal, would end up putting New York away.

The Hurricanes would win this series in six games. And despite a depleted forward group, they'd advance to the Eastern Conference Final before getting swept by the Florida Panthers. A trip to hockey's Final Four is a pretty good run, but if there's one thing about sports franchise ownership that Dundon seems to still be grappling with, it's that. A successful season still ends with a loss. Intellectually, it's reasonable to expect a Stanley Cup only 3 percent of the time. It's what he's planning on. That means 97 percent of the time another owner ends up on top. For someone who always believes he's going to win, who believes his methods are the path to success, that math is tough.

"It sucks. It's terrible. That's been the hardest part of this," he said.

His ownership will ultimately be judged on Stanley Cups. That's how it's always been done in hockey. So of course he disagrees.

"The team with the best winning percentage, that is how you should judge it," he said. "That's it. But that's not how it's judged.

"Hopefully, we get lucky."

CHAPTER 8

REVEALING THE VALUE IN PEOPLE

He taught us the difference between being alive and living.

—Brad Treliving

B rad Treliving pulled the rental Grand Cherokee with Florida plates into a parking spot at the Delamar Hotel in the resort town where we'd just had lunch and put it in park. We were winding down a conversation that had started in the lobby of this hotel, continued at a local joint called Bubba's, and wrapped up in a rental car. The Toronto Marlies team bus that would haul a group of Maple Leafs prospects to a rink ten minutes away was a few spots behind us.

Our final topic of conversation was Treliving's dad.

I'd known Brad Treliving for years as a smart, funny, thoughtful NHL executive who always took the time to help or do whatever he could to assist what I was working on. This is how he operates. It's how he interacted as a young defenseman in the ECHL, an unknown assistant GM of the Arizona Coyotes, a more well-known GM of the Calgary Flames, and it's how he interacts as the general manager of the Toronto Maple Leafs, in the center of the hockey universe.

"He's worked his way up," said Coyotes head equipment manager Stan Wilson, who got an up-close look of Treliving as he got his start as an NHL executive. "The guy was working in the Western Professional Hockey League. Now he's in the situation he's in. And he's helped other people on his way up. He's helped all the people around him. . . . The cool thing is I can text him right now and he'll text back in five minutes. He's the GM of the Maple Leafs. He doesn't need to text me back."

Really, he doesn't need to do anything.

We'd interacted for years before I discovered that his father, Jim Treliving, was a co-owner of Boston Pizza, on *Dragons' Den*, Canada's version of *Shark Tank*, and worth millions. I had no idea. None.

"Same with me! None of us did," said Shane Doan, who played for Treliving in Arizona and left working for the NHL to join him in Toronto as a special advisor. "I was with Hockey Canada. . . . At the World Championships, we'd won, and I came back from doing something, and I was talking with his dad and was like, 'Oh my goodness. It's *that* Treliving.' I was like, '*What?*'"

It's also true that his grandfather was a barber. And that his father originally left home to become a police officer. So, sitting in that SUV, winding down a lengthy conversation, it made sense when he started talking about what he learned most from his dad.

Some of it is about business. That's inevitable. He learned about the importance of vision. Of surrounding yourself with people who complement your skills. His dad's business partner was a chartered accountant. His dad was a dreamer, ready to change the world every day.

He also learned about sacrifice. He knew that he and his sister were the most important things in his dad's life, but his dad was also gone a lot while building the business.

"I've got a lot of respect for that," he said.

Still, that wasn't the most important thing.

When he was a kid, his dad would take him on four- or five-day-long trips where he'd drop in on the Boston Pizza franchises. He'd watch how his father interacted with the owner of the restaurant and how he'd interact with the staff. The respect was always the same. He asked them all questions, he tried to help all of them.

"He's as comfortable with the dishwasher and the guy taking out the garbage as he is with the president and CEO," Treliving said. "I really did learn that from him. It's the value of people."

That ability to connect with people may be Treliving's biggest strength. It's also something that would be tested immediately in his newest job. Less than four months before we met, Treliving had been named the GM of the Toronto Maple Leafs. There's no bigger GM job in hockey. It's like running the New York Yankees. He'd have the biggest budget, he'd have some of the best players in the world, and all the pressures that go with both.

It was also complicated. He'd walked away from his job as the GM of the Calgary Flames in a decision the usually forthcoming Treliving declined to elaborate on beyond being complimentary of those still there.

"We made a decision. The people are awesome," he said. "They were awesome to me. They afforded me an opportunity to come back, and it wasn't quitting on them. It wasn't, I'm going somewhere else. I just felt for that team to move forward and the things that had to happen, probably I had to move on."

In Toronto, it was just as confounding. One moment it looked like Kyle Dubas was headed for an extension. The next, he was fired by president Brendan Shanahan and the GM search was on. On top of it all, Dubas and Treliving are good friends. When it looked like the Maple Leafs job was a possibility, Treliving called Dubas to let him know he felt a bit weird about the whole thing, like cheating on someone.

"He was good. He was like, 'I hope you get it because I know you, I know the people there. I think you'd be great for them,'" Treliving said. "And then the process moved fairly quickly."

It was then that his people skills, his ability to immediately connect, everything he observed with his dad and inherited, needed to kick in. It was all a whirlwind. It was all just getting started.

"That's when you lean into your beliefs and your core values," he said.

Early on with the Maple Leafs, that's exactly what he did.

When we first walked into Bubba's in Traverse City, a lunch spot where we sadly did not order the twenty-four-ounce Bloody Mary that includes two shots of vodka, two onion rings, two chicken wings, and a Miller High Life, Treliving noticed something on the walls as we sat down that sparked a memory.

Over each of his shoulders was a shelf attached to the exposed brick wall with black pipes. The shelves had local beer taps screwed in side by side—Bell's, New Holland, Roak Brewing Co.,

Grand Traverse Brewing Company—and Treliving kicked right into a story. This is what he does best.

"So these taps . . ." he began.

It was early in his tenure with the Calgary Flames and he wanted to add size to his defense, so he brought Douglas Murray on a professional tryout. He told Murray that he wanted to negotiate his contract before the start of the tryout so that they weren't arguing over money if he made the team. He wanted the tough conversation to happen first. They went back and forth awhile on his deal and Treliving wasn't budging.

"He's like, 'You know what? I'll take what you're offering. Things are going okay for me outside the game,'" Treliving said. "He had patented—you know how you pour tap beer and then you turn it off and it runs another second or two and beer comes out? It doesn't seem like a lot, but he had it calculated. He goes to the owners of these bars and he's got a little plug or whatever, [it stopped] as soon as you hit stop. He patented it."

That was how our conversation over lunch started.

He wrapped and I asked how he's been.

"I've been okay. I've been okay," he answered. "It's been a little bit busy."

It was the first indication that he took a new job, aside from his black Maple Leafs quarter zip. It was the first indication that he'd jumped into the biggest GM chair in hockey in the middle of their offseason and spent the summer working from 6 a.m. to midnight. Usually in moments like this, when you're looking for insight it's best to have the benefit of time. Generally, people are much more apt to open up and share details about something that happened a decade ago than something that is still fresh. That still hadn't settled.

But the flurry of a transition in Toronto is a fascinating place to start because jumping into that scenario—intense scrutiny, pressure, and even a little weirdness—is kind of perfect for someone with Treliving's skills. He knew by jumping into the job in June he was already late. So he arrived with a thirty-day, sixty-day, and ninety-day plan to get through the first three months.

"Day one, I met with everybody for twenty minutes. Who are you? What do you do? Unless your house is on fire right now, get back to work. I'll see you in July," Treliving said.

He had roster decisions to make. He had to make a decision on coach Sheldon Keefe, someone as closely associated with Dubas as anyone in the organization. He wanted to get started on relationship building with Auston Matthews and William Nylander because their contracts would soon be a priority.

"And we had thirteen [unrestricted free agents]. And then we had a draft. It was all in three weeks," Treliving said.

To help the process, he brought in Doan as a special advisor. Immediately, Doan saw a frantic effort to make up for lost time in those earliest weeks. Treliving was en route to the office at 5:45 a.m. He was sending texts to Doan at midnight.

"He had to catch up. He had to catch up. All he kept saying is he needed more time," Doan said. "'There's only so many hours in a day, Tree.' He was doing everything. You hear stories of people doing that and I think at times it's almost busywork. People are trying to prove something. It wasn't with him. It was 'I'm behind. We have the draft coming. Free agency coming.' Had to make decisions. He was drinking from the fire hose there."

Treliving estimated that he might have said two words to Sheldon Keefe before taking the Maple Leafs job. This wasn't a coach he knew particularly well, other than he noticed he seemed to win a lot of games during the regular season. To get the assessment he needed as quickly as he needed, he tried to be as direct as possible with the coach he inherited. He was going to have to ask uncomfortable questions. To Treliving, there are a few traits that are nonnegotiable when it comes to his head coach.

The coach needs to be technically sound. They need to have a foundational agreement on how the game should be played. They need to be a strong communicator with the players because of how players have evolved. He's learned that through experience.

"Everybody thinks everything has to be butterflies and lollipops and it's not. There has to be communication. There's a certain way you have to treat people," Treliving said. "Then it's about fit."

He sees players with shorter attention spans now. So he's watching to see if a coach is still capturing the attention of the players, if there's accountability. He's also a believer that a change at coach is an effective way to capture the attention of the players. He was figuring out how much of this attention capturing was necessary because few things do it as effectively as a coaching change.

"It's like walking into your house, everything is the same and all of a sudden you change your room and everyone sits up a little straighter," he said. "You bring in a new coach and you get that bump."

They'd talk every day in a running conversation about how to build the team. They'd go through the roster. They dissected each player on an expiring contract. They'd watch film. When free agency opened, Keefe was an integral part of identifying fit, and the feedback Treliving got after they started signing players made an impression.

"The guys we went after, pretty much we got," Treliving said. "One of the consistent themes coming back, when the agent would phone and say, 'We're coming,' is that the players are really blown away with the conversation they had with Sheldon. There's depth to the conversation. He dug into their game, the good and the areas we can do better at and where he sees them playing, how they can fit in and how we play."

Treliving also spoke with current players.

"It's like your kids, you love your kids, but you don't necessarily take everything they say as gospel," Treliving said.

They liked Keefe. They said he pushed them. They gave examples where they worked through difficult situations. And lastly, Keefe still really believed in this team. Playoff disappointments or not. Treliving saw a genuine faith in the key players he felt was necessary.

"There's been some disappointments. There can be a time when you say, 'Oh fuck, these guys.' Right?" Treliving said. "He believes in them. I was like, 'Can you win with this group?' It wasn't like 'Ehhhh.' It was 'Yes. One hundred percent. One hundred percent. They're growing and we're learning and we've gone through hard lessons and we're still going through those things. No doubt in my mind.'"

There was no hedge. Keefe got a two-year extension later in the summer.

The conversations to get a contract done with franchise center Auston Matthews started even earlier. In Calgary, Treliving was burned by two star players leaving the team in Johnny Gaudreau's exit via free agency followed by Matthew Tkachuk's decision not to sign an extension, which led to the trade to Florida. So it was understandable that he'd want an indication of Matthews's plans before making any major career decisions. Wasserman's Judd Moldaver, who is Matthews's longtime agent, and Treliving have a strong relationship and the two chatted by phone in May while Treliving was weighing his next steps to get an understanding of where things stood between Matthews and the Maple Leafs.

"I said, 'Listen, Brad, he's going to play in Toronto barring something crazy,'" Moldaver said. "When Kyle got fired, it wasn't like 'Oh, we're out of here.' It was 'Oh, let's see who they hire.'"

On May 31, Treliving was announced as the next GM of the Maple Leafs. A day or two after getting the job, he flew to Phoenix to spend time with Matthews, to get to know him and his family quickly.

"You're speed dating," Treliving said.

When he arrived in Arizona, Treliving, Moldaver, Doan, Auston, and his father, Brian, met at a Scottsdale resort called Sanctuary for dinner. Surrounded by desert mountains, palm trees wrapped in white lights, and a private space at the resort's farm-to-table restaurant, Elements, they used the time to connect, share plans, and swap stories. By this point, Moldaver, picking at the Wild Isles salmon that night, said he made two things clear—Matthews's plan was to get a deal done before the season started, but not until after July 1, so he could see how the team was shaping up. There just needed to be a level of comfort with the new GM and where the franchise was headed.

"I worked in Phoenix when [Matthews] was growing up, so you had stories, right? It's just sort of the personal side, and then, 'Here's my thoughts on the team from the outside view,'" Treliving said. "Then you get to 'Hey, you're leading the bus here. I look at this as, this is a partnership.' I said to him, 'A lot of guys can go through their career and not have a player like [him]. . . .'

It was a responsibility for me to make sure he's surrounded with people."

Treliving and Moldaver met again over breakfast at the Four Seasons Hotel in Nashville during the week of the NHL draft in June and talked conceptually about the contract. This might have been a new project for Treliving, but Moldaver had a pretty good idea how he thought the deal should look.

"I was thinking about it for eighteen months," he said.

In early August, the two met again for an Italian meal at Ristorante Sotto Sotto in Toronto to continue the progress. They talked consistently by phone. Then, on August 22, Moldaver said he asked Treliving to be available the next day. From Matthews's home in Arizona the following afternoon, Moldaver and Matthews FaceTimed Treliving, ready to finish the deal.

"I said, 'Hey, Tree, I have the big boy here. We've had countless discussions. . . . We've had a lot of thought, we've contemplated everything,'" Moldaver said. "'All the things we've talked about, Tree, factoring in the everything of everything, we're prepared to agree to a deal right now and announce it today.'"

The deal would be for four years at an annual salary of $13.25 million. A new league high for average annual salary. They also wanted Matthews to be able to break the news on Twitter rather than have any of it leaked out to the media.

"He goes, 'Yes, it's a deal,'" Moldaver said. "That was it."

At 4:55 p.m. on August 23, Matthews tweeted, "I feel fortunate to continue this journey as a Maple Leaf in front of the best fans in hockey! I will do everything I can to get us to the top of the mountain. GLG!"

By the time we were chatting in September, two of the biggest storylines and potential distractions entering the season had already been removed, opening up more time for Treliving to do what he's always been known for by those who work for him or compete against him: obsessing over options to get better.

There is a story that has been passed down through the years among those in sports leadership. It's hard to say exactly where it originated, but the best I could find was in a conversation between boxing promoter Teddy Atlas and former NFL coach Bill Parcells. In a 2006 story in the *New York Times*, writer Michael Lewis relayed how much Parcells loved the story of middleweight boxer Vito Antuofermo and his upset win over Cyclone Hart in the 1970s. Hart was the heavy favorite in a match against Antuofermo. He had all the talent, all the quickness, and a big left hook.

Antuofermo counterpunched with resilience.

For four rounds, Hart was dominant. It was everything the crowd expected. But Antuofermo withstood it all and survived his way to the fifth round, when Hart showed his first signs of tiring. Antuofermo, the story goes, seized on the opportunity and delivered a series of quick punches that took down the heavy favorite.

The reason the story survives is because of a conversation after the match. A thin curtain divided the two fighters and Hart could overhear a conversation between Antuofermo and his cornermen, who were preparing to take him to the hospital. The underdog was in so much pain that he said if Hart had hit him with just one more left, he was going to quit. But he battled through and that final left never happened.

Hart heard this and wept. At least that's what Parcells told Lewis.

Years later, Alabama coach Nick Saban would get onstage and share a version of it.

"I may not even get the names of these two guys right," Saban said. And he wouldn't. Saban started out his version of the story by calling the underdog Arturo Freeman, who was actually a defensive back for the Miami Dolphins. The details weren't exact, but the message was the same. And that Saban message was what Treliving heard one day and it stuck with him.

"The point of the story is you don't know what your competition is going through," Treliving said when we chatted for *The Full 60* podcast following a general manager's meeting in Florida one year.

For Treliving, it inspired an attitude of relentless pursuit of improvement through work. As a GM, that means constant conversations with his colleagues with other teams. It often seems like Treliving's teams are attached to every big trade rumor. It's often true because he's constantly making those calls.

"I think he's just very methodical and thorough. He goes through everything at a slow pace, thinks everything through. The pros and cons of every player and every trade," said Derek Clancey, who played with Treliving in the ECHL and joined him in Toronto as an assistant GM. "He's always watching. I'm sure a lot of GMs do it. I think he dials in to watch his team needs. He's always watching those areas . . . always doing something productively towards making the team better."

His philosophy is that, unless he asks, he never knows what the opposing general managers are thinking. Unless you throw that last left hook, you never know you're one punch away from winning. Glen Gulutzan saw it up close when he was the head coach of the Calgary Flames and Treliving was his GM. What he appreciated about Treliving's management style was that he was inclusive in incorporating everyone on the staff. If he was having a million conversations with people around the league, he was having just as many with people inside the team in order to get their input.

"He is such a persistent worker," Gulutzan said. "He leaves no stone unturned. He really gets after it."

During one off day, Gulutzan woke up at 7:45 a.m., grabbed his phone, and saw that he had already missed seven calls from Treliving.

"I was like, 'What the heck does he have going?'" Gulutzan said.

In this instance, Treliving was in pursuit of signing Jaromir Jagr, and through his consistent conversations got word that the St. Louis Blues were making a push, so he was eager to get it done. Just keep throwing punches. The most memorable version of this for Gulutzan was Treliving's pursuit of Matt Duchene when Duchene was a young star center looking to get out of Colorado. Gulutzan estimated that for three consecutive months, they spoke every day about the possibility of acquiring Duchene. What were his strengths and weaknesses? Where would he fit in the lineup? What was it going to take to acquire him? As the deal started to take shape, Gulutzan spoke often with Treliving about every possible aspect of the deal. Colorado wanted a young defense-man named Juuso Valimaki as part of the package, and so they spent time dissecting exactly what the impact would be including a player they had recently taken with the sixteenth-overall pick in the draft.

If it was a game day, Treliving would wait for the morning skate to wrap and then head to the coach's office to go over every update. Then at the end of the night there might be a call wrapping up the day's work. If they were going to do this, everybody would know every detail.

"It was inclusive. We worked in tandem," Gulutzan said. "He always included me."

When it didn't feel right, he also knew when to stop. This trade ended up transforming the Colorado Avalanche in part because the team that acquired Duchene, the Ottawa Senators, gave up so much, including a draft pick that ended up being the fourth-overall pick in the 2019 draft (Bowen Byram). Gulutzan knew to expect multiple visits per day and to expect calls at all hours. This is a tricky balance to work as a leader of an organization. Done wrong it can be annoying. And while Gulutzan admits to sending a few of those calls to voicemail when he'd had enough, he also said Treliving walks the line well.

"He's got a great personality. He likes to laugh. He can make fun of himself. He doesn't take himself too seriously," he said. "What makes it non-annoying is he's inclusive. He's not jamming you. He's just working with you. That's the part I enjoyed."

"He creates an environment where you want to help," said Doan. "He makes you feel like he wants your help and that it will matter. That makes you want to do more."

It makes those texts at midnight tolerable. It makes the seven calls at wake-up in the morning understandable. He's constantly putting in the work, including others on the staff, and the result in one case was a relationship that would end up being life-altering.

It's always meant as a compliment. When you comment on some-body who has achieved new heights in their career, has risen to a level of prominence like, say, running the most valuable franchise in hockey, and point out that they haven't changed at all, that's usually a good thing.

People say that a lot about Brad Treliving. People who knew him back in the ECHL. Or who worked for him in the Texas minor leagues. Or interacted with him when he was the assistant GM of the Arizona Coyotes.

They say he hasn't changed because when they shoot him a text, he responds immediately despite countless demands on his time. They say it because, when they do meet up in person again, he reconnects immediately. He jumps right into a story, and there are few better at that in the game. But on a Thursday afternoon during a memorial for his close friend Chris Snow, his former assis-tant GM in Calgary, he let everyone seated in St. Michael Catholic Community know about a relationship he said changed him. It was a relationship with someone who changed so many he came across.

One of four speakers at Snow's memorial, Treliving carried sheets of paper up to the podium, straightened them out in front of him, fixed the microphone slightly, and then told the room just how much Snow had made an impact on him.

We come to celebrate an extraordinary man. . . .

The relationship between Snow and Treliving might exemplify one of Treliving's biggest strengths as a manager. Rod Pasma, vice president of hockey operations for the NHL, has known Treliving for decades. He worked with him when Treliving was running the minor hockey league in Texas. He's battled with him as the supervisor of a playoff series.

"To me, good leaders spend an inordinate amount of their time trying to make their employees, their players, their people better. Better at what they do. Better at life," Pasma said. "Tree was really good at that."

Snow didn't know any of this when Treliving was hired by Brian Burke and the Calgary Flames in the spring of 2014. Snow was driving through Scottsdale, Arizona, on vacation with his wife, Kelsie, when he got the news that he had a new boss. As someone who had made the rare transition from the media into a hockey front office, he wasn't thrilled. All he knew about Treliving was that he was going to have to prove himself to someone new all over again. And Treliving's first impression was Snow being out on vacation.

"In hindsight, his hiring was the best thing that Brian Burke could have done for my career," Snow said when we chatted in 2020. "When Tree came in, he was really good because he said, 'Okay, we're going to build the best analytical department in the league. Tell me how we're going to do that.'"

Each year, that department grew larger. Treliving and the Flames invested more in analytics. Not only that, Snow started to get more and more responsibilities under his new boss.

> When I got in and met Chris, we didn't have an analytics department. We didn't have a data department. He started all that. And it wasn't long after him being involved that he was not just involved in analytics, he was involved in everything.

Treliving once told Kelsie Snow that it didn't take him long to figure out that Chris was the smartest person in the room. Once that realization set in, the scope of his job expanded. Kelsie could tell that his responsibilities were increasing because of how busy he was at the most important times in the NHL calendar. Around the trade deadline, the calls from Treliving were relentless.

Treliving didn't come in, sweep out the old regime, and bring in his people. He developed the people he thought were the smartest and most capable of helping the team win. It was the same way he approached the staff in Toronto.

"The thing that Brad does well is identify somebody's skills and let them do that," Kelsie said. "He isn't afraid to invest emotionally in people, which I think can be a tricky thing in a lot of business circles."

In June 2019, right before the NHL draft in Vancouver, Snow was diagnosed with ALS. He was given one year to live. In a soul-crushing moment, Treliving said he'd never seen anything more impressive. Snow got the worst news of his life and forty-eight hours later was at work helping the Flames get ready for the draft. *Who are we going to draft? How are we going to get better?*

> It was at that time I saw Chris immediately not waste a free moment with his family. They flew to Vancouver for the draft. After the draft, we were all going to fly back to Calgary. Chris said, 'No, we're going to drive.' I said, 'It's an hour flight, it's about a twelve-hour drive. Let's do the math here.' He said, 'Brad? I'm going to take every moment I can to enjoy every moment I can.' He taught us the difference between being alive and living.

Snow always understood that he had a higher hurdle to clear than others in the game because he came up through journalism. His strategy was to put in the work, be open and honest with people about who he was and how he could help, and hope to earn their respect over time. He also wasn't scared to share his opinion. Treliving joked about his Boston brashness, how he and fellow Flames assistant GM Craig Conroy would get into battles over players with Conroy eventually trying to end the fight by reminding Snow that he was wrong because he didn't play the game. Snow would fire back that it was even worse for Conroy— he played the game and he was *still* wrong. The two would inevitably hug it out afterward.

Treliving let him help with contracts. Then he started doing the actual negotiations for contracts. Treliving joked that, at one point, it got heated enough between an agent and Snow that he thought the agent might come over the desk swinging. But this all happened because of Treliving's ability to develop a talented executive. Snow didn't arrive in Calgary fully formed. In fact, early on, he once apologized to Brian Burke for giving the appearance that he disagreed with him on a player evaluation. Burke ignored the apology and instead told him to always speak up with his player opinions. That confidence was heightened by Treliving.

"Brad saw him as somebody who was a hockey mind, who got it and didn't have to fight for that," Kelsie Snow said. "That allowed Chris to be himself in a way he hadn't been in his career."

By the time the Matthew Tkachuk trade came around in 2022, Snow was involved every step of the way. Kelsie remembers him at the lake in New Hampshire, sitting on a chair in a bathing suit with his head tipped back so his voice could be heard better. He spent hours on the phone that summer, running through every possible trade scenario involving Tkachuk, sending as much data as possible to Treliving for each of the scenarios.

"Chris was having the time of his life," Kelsie said.

The work meant so much to Snow. Like anyone, Treliving wondered if he was being a bad boss by loading up someone fighting ALS with work when every minute was counted. But this is what Chris loved. He loved his family. He loved hockey. He loved the action.

"He just absolutely was in his wheelhouse that summer. He loved every conversation," Kelsie said. "That's why he kept doing his job. It was so clear, it brought him so much joy. That was tied to Brad. Specifically, doing his job with Brad was a very important part of Chris's life."

When Treliving decided not to return to the Flames in April 2023, Kelsie said that he and his wife, Julie, visited their house to let them know in person, even though doing it that way made it almost impossible for everyone to keep it together. The next month, Treliving was starting a new job in Toronto. The two still kept in touch. The last text Snow sent to Treliving was one of optimism. Snow was busy learning new technology that would allow him to communicate. A no-click mouse. Head tracking to run a new iPad. An eye-gaze computer that he could operate completely with his eyes. Fear, he wrote to Treliving, had been replaced by excitement. *See you soon.*

Three days later, when Snow went into cardiac arrest and suffered a brain injury, Kelsie texted Treliving. *If you want to say goodbye to Chris, you have to come now.* Treliving flew out immediately. He spent time alone with him in the hospital. Snow died on September 30 at the age of forty-two. Like Kelsie, Treliving shared his emotions publicly during these times. She noticed him tearing up once during a press conference. She saw a vulnerability that wasn't always there in the past. She saw someone putting aside an insatiable work obsession for a friend.

To her, this was change, too.

"I think Chris being sick forced Brad to show that part of him," she said. "Showing vulnerability makes us appear stronger than weaker."

It was on full display during the eulogy.

Treliving's voice cracked slightly as he concluded, sharing what he thought Chris might advise him in a moment like this.

Mostly, Treliving suspected, he'd let them all know it was going to be okay.

CHAPTER 9

SERVING TO WIN

It's been life-changing. You talk about patience, that's when I realized what patience is.

—**Jim Nill**

Jim Nill was sitting by himself, watching the next great generational player compete against the Windsor Spitfires as a fifteen-year-old phenom. At this point, the world already knew Connor McDavid was special. I was in the building to work on a story for *ESPN the Magazine*, not exactly the media publication unearthing hockey prodigies. The secret was out.

But Nill *knew*. And he knew why.

I spotted him watching McDavid and worked my way down to his place in the stands. I'd get an honest evaluation from Nill without hype and hyperbole because he has seen a lot of great players at the earliest stages of their career. Also, hyperbole isn't part of the package with Nill. After he finished playing in the NHL, Nill got a job scouting for the expansion Ottawa Senators and was the organization's top scout when they drafted Daniel Alfredsson. When he was running drafts for the Detroit Red Wings, they extended their championship window by drafting Pavel Datsyuk, Niklas Kronwall, and Henrik Zetterberg. In running the Dallas Stars, Nill and his staff had a draft that was transformative for the franchise in landing a franchise defenseman, goalie, and goalscorer in the same class. And while in each of those cases he's always quick to credit someone else ("that one was all John Ferguson Sr.," "that one was all Håkan Andersson," "that one was all Joe McDonnell"), drafting and development success seems to follow him around.

So when you start hearing that this kid from Newmarket, Ontario, has the potential to be one of the all-time greats, Nill is exactly the guy you want to run it by. And so, in a half-filled rink in the fall of 2012, I sat next to him and asked for an assessment of Connor McDavid.

"He's a great skater. He's effortless," Nill said, looking ahead. "He's got great change of speed. He gets the puck and he's gone. He's got quick hands. He's one of those guys the puck just kind of follows."

Nill also mentioned his hockey IQ, which can mean different things to different people. McDavid was doing something that indicated he thought the game differently than the other teenagers. Nill provided an example.

"He made a play down here on the power play. Started to take it to the net and all of a sudden pulled back and made a pass to the guy back here in the slot. Most people would just be heading right to the net," Nill explained with his usual patience. "He just stopped and pulled back and got the guy a great shot. They have that second sense. The good players see the game as we see it up here. They can slow it down. When you're up here the game is real slow. You get down low by the glass, it's a blur. They have the sense of seeing the game up high and slowing it down. That's how Gretzky and Crosby are."

Nill, one of the most understated people you'll ever meet, was comparing a teenager to two all-timers. Of course, he'd be right.

Almost a decade later, Nill and I were sitting in the stands again, watching another group of prospects. This time, we were four hours northwest of that Windsor arena, taking in a tournament he helped create. We were watching his Dallas Stars prospects compete against the Toronto Maple Leafs in the annual Traverse City Prospect Tournament, one of a number of pre–training camp prospect tournaments being held around the NHL as summer starts turning into fall.

But this particular tournament was the first of its kind. And the man sitting to my left was one of the guys who came up with the concept. While he was with the Red Wings and the team was loaded with Hall of Famers winning back-to-back Stanley Cups, Nill and then-GM Ken Holland had a problem to solve. They'd bring recently drafted kids into their organization for training camp and they'd have to play against Steve Yzerman, Brendan Shanahan, Sergei Fedorov, and Nicklas Lidstrom. It's not an ideal situation in which to evaluate young players.

"It was impossible," Holland said.

They reached out to a few teams to see if they'd join them in Traverse City for a prospect tournament to help provide a better environment for evaluation, and this tournament became the launching point for some of the best players to play in the NHL during this era. It became a model copied all over the league.

"I remember [Ilya] Kovalchuk and [Dany] Heatley here, and

Jamie Benn and James Neal, they were here. Rick Nash, I just saw him and mentioned it to him," Nill said after running into Nash as an executive with the Columbus Blue Jackets years after watching him play in this tournament as a prospect.

He's been part of this tournament so long that the young players he had just addressed in the Dallas Stars dressing room were a little fuzzy in recognizing the big names that preceded them in using these games to propel their careers.

"I mentioned some of the players before, the history of the tournament, some of the big players like Kovalchuk—young kids don't know who those guys are," Nill said.

Then he let out a big laugh.

He was sixty-five years old and it was clear he still loved coming to the rink and developing careers. But as the GM of the Dallas Stars, Nill is like everyone else who works their way up as an executive. Every step higher is one rung farther away from doing what you loved first. So now Nill gets his satisfaction by developing those around him. There are a lot of different leadership styles that lead to success in running a professional sports franchise, but the one Nill excels at is leading by serving. Sometimes that means regular meetings in his office with a young lawyer to give her career advice as she chases the dream of one day running an NHL team, as he did for Alana Matthews, who eventually became the Dallas Stars' executive vice president of business operations. Or patiently sharing exactly how he scouts a game and spending hours together in a car talking with a young former agent who was rounding out his skill set in a hockey front office, as he did for Ryan Martin, now an assistant GM for the New York Rangers.

One evening in Martin's first year working with Nill in the Detroit Red Wings front office, Nill picked him up in his Chevy

Suburban, as he always did. They ate dinner at a place called Tunnel Bar-B-Q, as they always did. During the first period of the game, Martin was furiously taking notes on the action in front of him. Notes in the margins of the roster. Notes on his pad. Everything he saw, he recorded it somewhere in front of him. Occasionally he'd look out of the corner of his eye to see what Nill was doing and his eyes were always on the ice, only occasionally noting something on the small notepad in his hand.

"He's writing things like an old detective," Martin said.

At the end of the period, Martin finally asked him: What have you written down?

Nill responded with a question: Who did you like in that period?

Martin told him about a player on the opposing team who was on the puck a lot, who was extremely competitive. He jumped out.

"I show him my sheet and it's eighty other things about these other people," Martin said.

Nill showed him his detective pad. He noticed the same thing about that player. They both had the same conclusion, but Martin was frantically taking so many other notes that he lost focus of the most important thing. Years later, that lesson still stood out to Martin when talking about Nill.

"He's different. He's different than anybody else in hockey," Martin said. "I think he really enjoys developing people. In this business, there are a lot of people who are the opposite."

When we sat down to watch the Stars prospects, Nill and his Dallas Stars were coming off a trip to the Western Conference Final the previous season, their second time advancing at least that far in the last four years. They've succeeded like all Nill-led teams succeeded—drafting and developing. Then surrounding those players with the right veterans. But to characterize Nill for just his ability to recognize talent misses so much more.

———

Great success doesn't happen immediately. It's a series of small decisions that lead to something bigger. It's patience. It's resilience. It's developing a compass that points you toward the right goal and persevering through the obstacles that inevitably emerge. In 2017, the Dallas Stars had one of the greatest drafts in franchise history. It's too soon to crown it anything beyond that, but it's not unreasonable that it becomes an all-timer. In a matter of two days, the Stars acquired a franchise defenseman in Miro Heiskanen, a franchise goalie in Jake Oettinger, and a high-scoring winger in Jason Robertson, three of the toughest slots to fill on a championship roster. Pick one of those in a decade and that's an accomplishment. Two? You're setting yourself up for playoff success. Three in the same draft?

It just doesn't happen.

"That changed our franchise," Nill said. "These kids showed up and changed everything."

It all started with the signing of a forward who had scored a total of two NHL goals in the season before Nill decided to bring him to Dallas.

On July 1, 2014, the Dallas Stars signed unrestricted free agent Patrick Eaves to a one-year deal worth $650,000. Eaves had some pedigree. He was a first-round pick by the Ottawa Senators in 2003. He had a twenty-goal season on his record. His dad, Mike, played in the NHL and coached at Wisconsin. But his career had slowed because of injuries and he was starting to bounce around the league. Ottawa. Carolina. Detroit. Nashville. Now Dallas. Nill knew him well. Their time in Detroit overlapped. He liked Eaves because he was a hardworking player with high character. He could provide depth to a team that needed it and, even with his career spinning a bit, had some upside.

In 2016–17, Eaves rewarded Nill's bet. He had his best offensive year by taking advantage of ice time with stars Jamie Benn and Tyler Seguin. He piled up goals on the power play, continued to be a hard worker, and by the time the trade deadline arrived he was the target for contenders looking to bolster their lineup. In February of that season, trade talks between Ducks GM Bob Murray and Nill got serious. On February 24, a deal was announced. A conditional second-round pick went to the Stars in return for Eaves.

This is where the attention to detail gets important.

That second-round pick would become a first-rounder in 2017 if the Ducks advanced to the Western Conference Final that spring *and* Eaves played at least 50 percent of the games in rounds one and two. The detail is even more minute. There was debate between the two teams about the particulars of those conditions. The Ducks wanted the condition to be that Eaves had to play 50 percent of the games in the first round and 50 percent of the games in the second round for the pick to be upgraded. Nill insisted that the deal be 50 percent of the cumulative games.

"To Jim's credit, Jim fought for that," said Stars assistant GM Mark Janko. "We got the second first-round pick [in 2017] because Jim fought for it to be cumulative."

Eaves played every game of the Ducks' first-round sweep of the Calgary Flames. But he injured his foot in Game 3 of the second-round series against the Edmonton Oilers, knocking him out for the rest of the playoffs. In all, he'd play seven games of the Ducks' first two rounds, just enough to trigger the condition to send the Ducks' first-round pick to the Stars. Had the Ducks won the condition debate, it would have remained a second-rounder, since Eaves only played three of seven games in round two.

Luck, as it often does in hockey, also played a part in that 2017 draft. Based on pre-lottery odds, the Avalanche or Canucks should have earned the top pick. But the New Jersey Devils jumped from fifth to first. The Philadelphia Flyers jumped from thirteenth to second. And Nill's Stars jumped from eighth overall to third. But not everyone who got lucky cashed in the way the Stars did. Heading into the draft, they were debating defensemen Cale Makar and Miro Heiskanen for their top pick. The man who has been by Nill's side for so much of his draft success, Joe McDonnell, couldn't shake a comparison when he debated whether to take Heiskanen.

"I said I thought he looked like Nick Lidstrom at the time," McDonnell said. "We went Miro over Makar. We're still ecstatic over that pick."

With the pick they acquired from the Ducks, Nill and McDonnell knew they wanted to go with a goalie because they felt that Jake Oettinger was special. Nill also started to pick up intel that he might not slip to twenty-ninth, where the Stars were picking. On the draft floor, McDonnell turned to him and added urgency. He thought they should trade up to make sure they got Oettinger. This decision to trade up was aided by Nill's ability to network and acquire information.

"What he would do would be sniffing around the week or so before the draft, trying to find out whether that's through other management, scouts, goalie coaches, agents—he would try to figure out all that stuff. He does it on the down-low, but he does it with a strict purpose," Janko said of Nill. "There's definitely an objective there. He now knows that he wants Oettinger. Am I going to have to move up? How hard do I have to move up?"

They found a willing partner in the Chicago Blackhawks and sent picks twenty-nine and seventy for the twenty-sixth overall pick. They got their man and their franchise goalie. They also weren't done.

On the second day of the draft, Nill and McDonnell homed in on another player: Kingston Frontenacs winger Jason Robertson. And as much as they wanted Robertson, they decided to sit tight with the thirty-ninth pick rather than make another move up. There were concerns about Robertson's skating that were circulating around the league, so they made a bet that he would slip. Which he did.

Four years later, he posted the first of back-to-back forty-goal seasons.

So much went into that transformative draft. Giving a guy like Eaves a shot and then maximizing the return when it was time to move on. Doing the research to know the goalie you covet likely won't be there when you pick, but the forward you love likely will. A little lottery luck. And a deep trust that has formed over the years between Nill and those who work for him. That trust would pay off again when the Stars drafted Wyatt Johnston based on just a few viewings and a slew of background work by McDonnell. In that situation, the Stars were able to trade down and still get Johnston. Nill can make the big-picture moves, moving down to stockpile picks, and still get the player they want because he trusts his staff.

Especially McDonnell.

The two first met while living in the Vancouver hotel Century Plaza together during the Canucks' 1982 run to the Stanley Cup Final. They were both young, quiet kids finding their way in the NHL and finding themselves on the biggest stage in hockey. In one memorable moment during that playoff run, the Canucks were playing the Chicago Blackhawks and every call seemed to go the other way. In a moment of frustration, coach Roger Neilson grabbed Nill's stick, draped a white towel over it, and waved it in mock surrender. Neilson was ejected.

"He was sitting there going, 'That's my stick,'" McDonnell said, recalling the moment.

When he thinks of Nill during those times, he thinks of a player who was ultracompetitive, who would do anything for his teammates. He also had a sneaky left that came in handy during fights, his time as a willing fighter the juxtaposition to his career now as a patient, thoughtful executive.

"He was wiry tough," McDonnell said. "He was tough as nails for his size. He was a quiet guy who just worked his tail off."

As their careers in hockey shifted to the world of scouting, McDonnell saw that competitive drive and work ethic up close. The two worked together for the Detroit Red Wings when McDonnell was hired to work for Nill in 1995. With Nill running the draft, McDonnell on the road, and superscout Håkan Andersson in Europe, the trio rattled off a run that extended the Red Wings Stanley Cup contention another decade. In 1998, the Red Wings added Pavel Datsyuk in the sixth round.

"We have to give that to Håkan," McDonnell said.

The following year, they selected Henrik Zetterberg in

round seven. Again, Andersson played a leading role, since he got tipped off by former Red Wing Anders Eriksson, who played with Zetterberg's brother. But Nill definitely gets the assist. Nill went to see Sweden's U18 team, mostly to get a close look at a kid named Mattias Weinhandl, and came away impressed with the player who would eventually become a Red Wings captain.

"There was this little skinny guy always on the puck. Always on the puck. Håkan Andersson is with me and he liked him, too. I said we have to keep an eye on this kid," Nill said. "We drafted him in the [seventh] round. It's not like we were crazy about him, but there was something there, and bingo. Two years later he's playing in the Olympics for Sweden."

The next draft? The Red Wings nabbed Niklas Kronwall in the first round to give the Red Wings a new young core. Those three drafts followed a stretch where the franchise missed often in not drafting a regular. But it was classic Nill: don't lose patience with the things you believe in the most, and have a little faith it's going to work out.

"You're not always right all the time, but if you stick with it, stick with your beliefs and your philosophies, it works out," Nill said.

The work required isn't easy. Or even safe. In an *ESPN the Magazine* article about Nill and his draft record, Lindsay Berra wrote that, while out scouting players, Nill once "shuffled across a Siberian tarmac in a snowstorm with an armed escort while a lone worker de-iced the prop plane's wings with a bucket of hot water, a stepladder and a broom."

McDonnell remembers spending twelve hours in a Moscow airport during a snowstorm when their flight was finally canceled.

The moment the flights were wiped out for the night, it became a race against others in the airport to the closest hotel. Nill, wearing dress shoes, battled through the clear disadvantage.

"There's two feet of snow on him and he's slipping and sliding," McDonnell said.

When they arrived, as understated as always, Nill turned to McDonnell.

"I shouldn't have worn these dress shoes."

Another time in Russia, they boarded a train and realized they had tickets for the wrong date. Whoever booked the tickets had entered the year incorrectly. So Nill and the scouts improvised when the conductor came looking for tickets.

"He stuffed everyone into a baggage compartment," McDonnell said. "Only one guy got kicked off the train. Just a lot of crazy stories out of Russia."

Like getting pulled over by Russian police for no other reason than the police were looking for a payoff.

"Nothing fazes him," McDonnell said before correcting himself slightly.

"Really, deep down it does," he said of his longtime friend. "He doesn't let it out at all. He's the most competitive guy you want to see. In our over forty-one years, I have seen him over that time, three times where he came in and it was just him and I and he was upset, he was mad, and he wanted to go back to his playing days and take this guy out. They're few and far between. He will never, ever let it out. . . . Even when you're in a losing streak, I'll give him a call, 'Just seeing how you're doing.' 'All's good. All's good.' We could lose eight in a row and 'All's good.'"

That steady presence ended up being crucial during one of the Stars' most improbable playoff runs.

The NHL's 2020 COVID playoff bubble has been described this way by many people who experienced it: it was a once-in-a-lifetime event that they'd never want to do again. There were two hub cities for the playoffs that started in August, Edmonton and Toronto. Because the Stars began in Edmonton and kept winning, it meant sixty-six days of seclusion in the same city.

They were sequestered from families. Stuck in the same routine. And in Jim Nill, they had just about the perfect leader to guide them through it.

Playoffs in the bubble were an absolute roller-coaster ride for those on-site. There were highs—a huge overtime playoff goal to win a game. There were lows—news from back home about kids acting up or someone getting sick and the helplessness that comes with not being there to assist. There was also boredom, lots of boredom. The Stars were staying at the JW Marriott attached to Rogers Place in Edmonton. Management was allowed to go from their hotel room to one team meeting room. They could walk to the arena, where there was a single restaurant open for teams to attend, along with two other restaurants at the hotel. There was COVID testing every day, alternating the throat swab with the swab up the nose. In the concourse of the arena, pickleball nets became home to epic battles between team staff. Julien BriseBois and Mathieu Darche playing for Tampa. Jarmo Kekalainen and Bill Zito for Columbus. Marc Bergevin and Scott Mellanby for Montreal. Sometimes, a barber was allowed on the concourse and people in the bubble would line up for a haircut. There was a small area outside that led to food trucks. It was contained by fences, and team members joked that it felt like a prison yard.

Try not to get shanked by the Golden Knights on the way to grabbing a coffee.

In the chaos, Nill saw opportunity. He'd tell his group that not every team got this chance to see opposing players live and up close. Some days, there were three games to watch and it made for a fascinating petri dish of scouting for the teams that advanced. With every round the Stars won, Nill believed they were getting an advantage over other teams in building for the future. The Lightning, who played the Stars in the Stanley Cup Final that year, felt the same way.

Tampa built a war room in their Toronto hotel suite that had depth charts for every organization playing. They studied them closely and used the sequestered time together to get better.

"If we're watching the Rangers and Carolina, in our suite between periods it's 'Okay, why are the Rangers so good? Why is Carolina so good? How do they get to this team? What's missing from them and what can we learn from that?'" BriseBois said. "Tremendously valuable experience just watching what other teams are doing, how they got to where they are, why they're successful, why they're not."

The Stars took the same approach, a natural conclusion for someone like Nill with scouting drive coursing through his veins. But that wasn't his biggest contribution. It was his presence. Talk to enough people about Nill, and one common thread emerges. He's remarkably steady. He's the same in the middle of a seven-game winning streak as he is during a seven-game losing streak. Steve Greeley, who joined the Stars in 2022 as director of strategy/scouting and development, remembers watching his first game with Nill as an employee with the team. When the Stars scored a goal, he looked over at Nill, who allowed the slightest of celebrations, a nearly imperceptible fist pump with his left hand.

The patience, the steady presence, the deep bonds with those around him—it isn't accidental. His approach to his job is very intentional, driven by something that goes beyond trying to win a Stanley Cup.

———————

The game in front of us had ended, the last of the games that night during the Traverse City prospect tournament. The players filed off the ice, walking back toward the locker rooms. The fans left, but we were still seated on the top row of a small seat of bleachers. Scouts and executives from other teams started exiting the rink behind us and those who saw Nill all offered a quick hello. Nill spotted Maple Leafs team president Brendan Shanahan, who won three Stanley Cups as a player on Red Wings teams Nill helped build, and lit up.

"Hey, big guy, how are you doing? Good to see you!"

Shanahan immediately stopped and the two caught up. Shanahan had just finished a summer overseeing a very public change in management from Kyle Dubas to Brad Treliving. Any difficulty that came with the transition disappeared in that moment and the fascination that came with getting a new set of eyes on the organization was very clear. He shared some of that process with Nill.

"It's like you're getting an audit," Shanahan said.

They chatted for a while. Shook hands, and Shanahan exited out the door down the hall. A moment later Red Wings assistant GM Kris Draper appeared. Draper and Nill got to know each other well, first with Draper as a player, and later when he entered the Red Wings front office.

"See you guys!" Draper waved as he walked by. Nill noticed Draper carrying workout gear and couldn't help taking a shot as he exited.

"Is that workout gear? Who are you giving it to?"

Draper let out a big laugh on his way out. As they left, I realized that we might be among the last few people in the building. Even the Zamboni driver was doing his final laps on the ice. Once the Zamboni engine shut off, the sound of the doors slamming shut behind it echoed throughout the rink. Then it was just the pure, chilled quiet that only comes in an empty rink with a large sheet of ice.

We'd been chatting awhile. We talked about scouting. About his start in management. About finding young players like Henrik Zetterberg and Niklas Kronwall and how the Stars' Class of 2017 might have changed the path of his franchise. There was really no comfortable transition to discussing something as deeply personal as his faith. But it felt necessary here. It affects the way he acts, the decisions he makes in his life, the way he treats other people. The patience he shows in just about every situation that is put in front of him.

"I'm not sure how comfortable you are talking publicly about your faith. . . ."

I paused a moment. It wasn't really a question, I was kind of hoping he would bail me out. He did.

"Yeah, I'm very comfortable. It's been life-changing," he said. "You talk about patience, that's when I realized what patience is. God is patient with me. I always believed in God, but I didn't know anything, didn't understand it."

When he was in his late forties, he connected with a small group of men at his church, and that friendship transformed his faith.

"My wife has been praying for twenty-three years for that to happen," Nill said.

His wife, Bekki, comes up in nearly every conversation about Jim. Their partnership in helping others is so intertwined that people usually mention her in the same breath as Jim when asked to share stories.

"Him and his wife, Bekki, are first-class individuals that put others ahead of themselves," said Rich Peverley, who played for Nill and is now player development coordinator for the Dallas Stars.

"I'm a huge Jim and Bekki fan and his family," said Alana Matthews, the team's former executive vice president.

"Bekki, his wife, is like an angel on earth," said Janko, the Stars' assistant GM.

"I was there with them for nine years, you don't think of Jim without Bekki," said Sharks assistant GM Tom Holy. "They're a unit."

She's central to the story. She's also the only reason he took the job in Dallas to begin with.

After missing the playoffs for four consecutive seasons, Stars owner Tom Gaglardi was looking to make a change at general manager in 2013. Team president Jim Lites asked Les Jackson, a longtime Stars executive, to put together a list of top replacements for Joe Nieuwendyk as the team's GM.

When Jackson presented a list to Lites, Jim Nill wasn't on it.

"If I can get Jim Nill, where would he be on the list?" Lites asked Jackson.

"If you can get Jim Nill, you don't need a list," Jackson answered.

Lites knew how entrenched Nill was in Detroit because of their time working together with the Red Wings. Lites also knew he was a favorite of Red Wings owner Mike Ilitch and that he was being paid more than some general managers, even though he was an assistant GM. But at one point, when Lites was working with a group that wanted to buy the Atlanta Thrashers, he connected with Nill to see if he'd be interested in joining that front office if it happened. Nill was interested. Those conversations led Lites to believe that he could lure him away from Detroit now that the Stars had an opening. His contract had also changed.

"About two or three years previously, we had struck a deal between Mr. Ilitch, Jimmy Nill, and myself that paid him pretty handsomely in terms of an assistant GM, probably the highest paid," Holland said. "In return, we could deny any team asking permission to hire him. In that three-year window, there were a number of calls to interview him that we denied per our right. When that deal was up, I understood he wanted to be an NHL GM. We negotiated a clause whereby if somebody called, we would grant permission."

Navigating contractual obligations with a billionaire owner intent on keeping him would end up being the smallest of obstacles Nill would deal with during this time.

Bekki Nill was first diagnosed with breast cancer as a thirty-seven-year-old in 1999. She has a picture of her liver from 2011 that she occasionally will show doctors so they understand just how big a fight she's been in since her cancer returned. When we chatted, she had just shown the picture to a doctor a few months earlier.

"He looked at it and was just shocked," she said. "He said, 'I've never seen anything as bad. I don't know how you're living.' I get that every time."

In 2011, she was diagnosed with stage 4 metastatic breast cancer that had spread to her shoulder, liver, ribs, and bones. Her recovery became the family's priority. Making sure she was getting the best possible care and had stability trumped any career aspirations Nill had at that point. So much so that when the Stars reached out to hire him, and he relayed it to his wife, he let her know he'd already decided he wasn't going to pursue the job.

"I am very, very sick, but I am at a peaceful place. They've told me I'm dying. There's a point where you're shocked—'I'm too young'—you go through all the things in your head," Bekki said. "I got to a place where I don't have control over this. I want to get up and enjoy the day and do what I can do. There was an acceptance. I would never have wanted him to not pursue his dream."

You *have* to go do that interview, she told him.

The Nill family is a family of deep faith surrounded by people of deep faith. Lisa Ilitch Murray, daughter of Mike Ilitch, started picking Bekki up and taking her on the forty-five-minute drive to her church, Mt. Zion, in Clarkson, Michigan. They were there to pray over Bekki, anoint her with oil, plead for healing. But as Bekki and Jim often do, Bekki was thinking of someone else as others were trying to help her. In the front of the church, there were prayer baskets where visitors could drop the names of loved ones needing specific help. One of the baskets was specifically for jobs. At this moment, Nill had one of the most lucrative contracts for an executive in his position, for one of the most successful franchises in hockey. And still, Bekki started dropping his name in that basket. She thought maybe that new job might be in ministry because of how deep Jim's faith had grown. But she also believed it wasn't in her hands. When he came to her and said he had a new job opportunity, she believed this was the response. This entire time, Nill had no idea his wife was praying for him in this way. Not until he told her about the Stars offer.

"I sat down with Bekki and said, 'You know what? It's a great opportunity to go to Dallas, but with your illnesses, you have great doctors, support of the Ilitches, I'll have a job for life there. Do I want to shake this up?'" Nill said. "She looked at me and said, 'We're going. That's God's calling.'"

That changed the mission. When Nill let Ilitch and the Red Wings know he was leaving, there was disappointment, but also an understanding that this was something he had to do. To them, it was an inevitability.

"Jimmy had been very patient," Holland said. "You just knew at some point in time, it was Jimmy's turn."

Nill wants to win in Dallas. He's a deeply competitive person. He knows what it's like to win a Stanley Cup and wants to share that feeling with those around him who haven't experienced it. But the job has developed into something deeper.

"I've been put in this position," Nill said. "I want the team to do well, but is there a way in doing that through a relationship with God where I can help change—get good people in there, help people who are going through things? That's kind of the attitude I've taken."

These stories, more than uncovering a future Hall of Famer in Sweden, are the stories that make Nill especially unique. Like the year when the Stars started the season 1–6–1. It was a terrible start and they were in the middle of a road trip through the Midwest.

San Jose Sharks assistant GM Tom Holy worked for the Stars at the time in public relations. During these trips to the Midwest, Holy often used it as a chance to catch up with his parents. Mired in that deep well of losing, Holy was visiting quietly with his mom and dad in the team's hotel in Pittsburgh. Nill walked over and joined the conversation.

"He sat with my mom and dad for an hour and fifteen minutes. Shared his life, perspective, talked about me. Made them feel more connected," Holy said. "When you're in hockey, you go and leave and work, and he made everybody a part of that. He made sure the people giving up their sons and daughters know what they're giving them up for."

Years later, Holy's mom would have a stroke. Days were much harder following the stroke, but that conversation came up often when Holy talked to her.

"That's the impact he has on people," Holy said.

Dallas assistant GM Mark Janko suffers from a condition called eosinophilic esophagitis that leads to inflammation of the esophagus, forming ridges where food can get lodged. During the second round of the playoffs in the bubble, the Stars lost a heartbreaker in Game 3 to drop their series lead to 2–1. They had a team meal back at the hotel—steak and rice. Food got caught in Janko's throat.

"It was bad. Bad bad," he said. "I was terrified."

He could breathe, but struggled constantly as doctors and trainers attended to him. His body was trying to reject food he didn't know was lodged. Eventually he went to his room, battling through it.

"Jim sat right in my small little room with me until about three thirty in the morning," Janko said. "He basically said,

'You've got to go to the hospital.' I was in tears, most traumatic thing in my life. Jim Nill was right there. Just after we lost Game 3 of the second round of the playoffs. He was so focused on me."

Janko ended up having the food surgically removed, discovered the cause, and got medication. It hasn't happened since.

"When adversity comes, that's when Jim's at his best," Janko said.

On February 15, 2021, an emergency alert went out to people in Dallas. The managers of Texas's electrical grid were ordering rotating outages. An ice storm hit the city and the power grid wasn't prepared. More than four million people lost power. Frozen pipes burst everywhere. Alana Matthews was executive vice president of business operations and general counsel for the Dallas Stars at the time, and mother of two boys under three years old, including her seven-month-old Thatcher. At the outset of the storm, she received a text from Nill.

"Bekki and I are thinking of you, you have a young baby. Do you have power?"

Their power loss was intermittent. She let him know that they were going to be fine. But it wasn't just a single courtesy text. Jim and Bekki kept checking in. Eventually Alana and her husband's home lost power for good. They lost heat. The temperature started to drop, so the family bundled inside in winter clothes. They piled on blankets. After resisting the initial help, they gave in to the invitation from the Nills.

Come stay with us.

The Nill home didn't have water, but it had heat. A pipe burst in their house and Nill had already cut open the ceiling and repaired it. Then they opened their home to a neighbor in need.

Since they have grandkids, their house was equipped with a crib and small nursery area. But it wasn't just offering up his home that stays with Matthews. It's the picture of Nill sitting next to her two-year-old son, Declan, and working on a puzzle. And then coloring. And then playing a little game of kickball. Sometimes doing it while holding her seven-month-old.

"He has no airs. He is all about people and taking care of people," Matthews said. "They give so much. They kept us safe through that storm."

They do this for anyone they come across. Because of the condition of her liver, Bekki Nill said she doesn't like to take any drugs during surgery. Instead, she uses time during surgery to chat with the doctors performing it.

"I know that's not normal," she said.

Once, a doctor mentioned he had a baby who needed care, but he didn't have any family in the area. In the middle of the surgery, Bekki offered herself and Jim up as babysitters.

"He just stops. 'You'll babysit?' He says, 'How will I get ahold of you?'"

She explained that her husband was in the waiting room and has been through this so many times that he won't be surprised at all when the doctor asks for their cell number. She joked that he might even have a business card at this point that says, "Yes, my wife will babysit."

"Jim is the same way," Bekki said. "Any players who get hurt. He's ditching me to be with that player. He knows I'm fine. He knows he needs to reassure that family. That person, that wife, and to be with them. We just balance each other out."

Matthews shares a story of a longtime Stars season ticket holder who died suddenly of a heart attack. She'd lost her mom at a young age, so she felt a pull to attend the funeral service, and she let the Stars staff know that she would represent the organization at the service. The Stars were covered. When she got there, she noticed Nill sitting quietly in the back, paying respects to a fan who cared so much about the teams he assembled.

"Those are the things he does that people don't know about," she said. "He puts in the work all the time. He is constant. He's a constant force for good."

"I've been in the NHL for twenty-five years. I've never met a better person than Jim Nill," Janko said. "He's selfless, humble, kind, generous, wise—it sounds like I'm biased because I work for him. If he fired me today, I would say the same thing. He's a leader of people."

In 2022, Nill decided not to renew the contract of Rick Bowness, the coach who helped guide the Stars to the Stanley Cup Final. This is a former teammate. A man Nill had gotten to know well. And still, when it comes time to make a tough decision, Nill makes it. Leading with empathy isn't avoiding difficult decisions, it's letting people know where they stand.

"That's the one job I left with zero hard feelings," Bowness said. "That's how much trust I have in him."

Those decisions never get easier over time. I asked Nill if it leads to sleepless nights in the days leading up to the decision, and he said he agonizes well before then. When is the right time? How do you deliver it? Is there any way to avoid it? But live your life a certain way and even the toughest decisions in hockey come with a little peace. You learn that even the mistakes, they help shape you.

"People always talk about experience, 'Oh yeah, at sixty you have experience.' It's true," Nill said. "You wish you could have that wisdom and experience when you're forty-five and you'll make different decisions, but God's journey is you have to live that. He's not going to give it to you. . . . You need to find out on your own, and that's going to make you a better person for it."

CHAPTER 10

HOW TO BUILD A FRANCHISE

I'll never look at the Stanley Cup the same again.

—George McPhee

It was a couple of days before the Vegas Golden Knights' season opener to defend their 2023 Stanley Cup and the entire team gathered on a private outdoor terrace next to a large swimming pool glimmering with the reflection of the Wynn casino in Las Vegas. It was a festive October evening, with summer still lingering enough that it reached ninety degrees earlier in the day. In two days, they would raise the banner on their 2023 Stanley Cup championship, closing the book on previous accomplishments to start working toward the next one.

But that night, the celebration was on. The players and staff would be getting their championship rings earned by beating the Florida Panthers in six games the previous June. I was assigned to table number nine, tucked away in the back near the pool and farthest away from the stage in front of us, where the proceedings would take place. After an hour of cocktails and photos taken with the Stanley Cup, we were asked to take our seats. I listened in to some of the conversation at our table and this was a group with intimate knowledge of the rings about to be handed out. I introduced myself to the guy sitting to my right.

"Are you with the jeweler?" I asked.

"I *am* the jeweler," he answered.

His name was Jason Arasheben and he owns Jason of Beverly Hills, a company that has designed championship rings for the Los Angeles Lakers, Tampa Bay Buccaneers, and, most importantly on that night, the Vegas Golden Knights. He and his team at my table were eager to see the reaction of the rings being delivered that evening. They were curious to see how the player reaction compared to NBA players, who celebrated each ring delivery with hollering and shots downed in celebration. For Jason, the coolest reaction of all was witnessing Tom Brady open his final Super Bowl ring.

Glasses of red and white wine were being refilled so dutifully that it became a running joke at our table that perhaps the staff was being paid by the glass. The jewelers also noticed all the beer bottles on the tables around us, which isn't usually the drink of choice for a ring ceremony in professional sports. The hockey players and their consumption tastes immediately endeared themselves to table number nine. Onstage, there was a four-piece band mixing jazz standards with songs like Harry Styles's "Watermelon Sugar," Rihanna's "Umbrella," and Dua Lipa's "Levitating." The Stanley Cup was at the center of the stage, flanked by the Clarence S. Campbell Bowl and Conn Smythe Trophy, which was awarded to Jonathan Marchessault, one of the Vegas originals, sitting a couple of tables over.

The food was amazing. Each plate delivered in exact unison by the waitstaff to everyone at the table. When the staff first brought out plates made of ice with a lobster tail, giant shrimp, and crab, someone at our table wondered out loud: "Each of us gets one of these?"

That was just the appetizer. A succulent cut of steak was paired with mushrooms, carrots, creamy spinach, and whipped potatoes. For dessert, everyone got their own chocolate Stanley Cup, the bowl filled with a chocolate liquid the waitstaff poured over the rest of the dessert. It was a bit of decadence in a night full of it. While we ate, people from the organization went onstage to speak. Golden Knights owner Bill Foley's son Robert let all the players know that they had their own personalized bottle of aged bourbon sitting underneath their chairs. That got big cheers. Then team president George McPhee walked from his table up front to the stage, facing all the players he helped acquire. He was filling in onstage for Bill Foley, who had to pull out at the last second for reasons McPhee only explained as an upper body injury. McPhee was hired as the franchise's first GM in 2016, and on the night he was handed a box containing a championship ring, the hiring seemed obvious. It wasn't.

In 2014, McPhee had been fired as the GM of the Washington Capitals after seventeen years without winning a Stanley Cup. He built the Capitals into a high-octane, talented team centered around superstar Alex Ovechkin, but it was also one that couldn't win in the playoffs. People questioned McPhee's coaching hires. They questioned his wisdom of building around a Russian winger who wasn't the prototypical team leader. They questioned whether the group McPhee assembled could ever get past Sidney Crosby and the Pittsburgh Penguins. When Foley bought the team, he made the declaration that his franchise would be a playoff team in three years and a Stanley Cup winner in six, something McPhee never accomplished in Washington. Complicating things further, on the day McPhee's hire was announced in 2016, the expansion draft was less than a year away.

"No one even knew Las Vegas was going to get a team," current Vegas GM Kelly McCrimmon said years later. "George got hired in the middle of July, I got hired the first of August, and we drafted our team in June, okay? . . . Fuck, we had eleven months, man."

They had eleven months, but McPhee had nearly two decades to develop a leadership strategy that was refined through successes, mistakes, and decisions he wanted to redo. He'd learned what was negotiable with a team owner and what was not. He learned where he could compromise with players and coaching hires and where he could not.

Some of these lessons he learned on his own. Some he discovered by taking advantage of a network with a depth of experience that comes with being an NHL general manager.

One offseason early on in McPhee's tenure as the GM of the Washington Capitals, Brian Burke invited him and a few other NHL executives to go on a fishing trip. They traveled to a fishing lodge on Langara Island, a remote outpost in British Columbia, just below Alaska. It's remote enough that it requires a helicopter to visit and the area is a refuge for wildlife, from humpback whales to bald eagles to grizzlies. Step into the fishing boat and you're surrounded by pristine pines and an expanse of deep blue water filled with halibut and, when McPhee fished, an abundance of coho salmon. On one of the days, he found himself sharing a boat with Harry Sinden, who had won a Stanley Cup as the Bruins coach in 1970 and spent decades in the Bruins front office. McPhee always admired Sinden and the way he operated.

"He was like Columbo to me," McPhee said.

McPhee noticed during general manager meetings that when the GMs would get into a passionate debate about a rule change or issue in hockey, NHL commissioner Gary Bettman wouldn't let the debate end until he asked Sinden for input. Usually Sinden spent most of his time listening to the debate rather than joining in.

"Gary Bettman would turn to him and say, 'What do you think, Harry?' And he'd give a completely different spin that I don't think anybody thought. It was amazing how many times he did that," McPhee said.

As they talked on the private fishing boat miles away from civilization, with Sinden sitting in back and McPhee up front, something compelled McPhee to get up and move from the front of the boat to the seat immediately beside Sinden. As he retold the story, McPhee got up from behind his desk and sat next to me to show the impact of changing proximity, to show the intimacy that's created when you move closer to be completely present as someone is telling their story.

"I just sat beside him," McPhee said. "Just like this. And he sort of looked at me, I don't know. I don't know how to describe it. It meant a lot to me and I knew it meant something to him. And then we just started talking more hockey and everything else and I was just asking him questions."

McPhee had a private boat with access to someone whose

playing career went back to junior hockey in Oshawa in the late 1940s. Who won an Olympic silver medal in 1960. Who coached the greatest defenseman to play the game in Bobby Orr. Who guided Canada to a victory in the 1972 Summit Series. The immense respect McPhee clearly has for those who did the job before him made for a natural connection, and his conversational style—soft-spoken with a willingness to be vulnerable—only enhances that connection. He was learning lessons in Washington, but he was also learning lessons from those around him.

"You learn from all the great people in this game. That's who you learn from. The Pat Quinns. The Bob Gaineys. The Lou Lamoriellos. You listen, you learn, you ask questions," McPhee said. "They feel respected when you ask questions."

It's also how he manages. He wants similar people around him. People who can connect. Who can ask the right question or provide an insight. As a leader, he wants to be the one guiding the conversation, not necessarily making every decision.

"It's just connecting with people. Connecting with people in the right way and not being overbearing. Not standing out. None of that," he said. "I like sort of just blending in with everybody else. I like a real participative style of management where, when you're in the war room with everybody, you lead off the meeting, but then the whole group takes over."

On the night of the ring ceremony, with the sound of helicopters giving Vegas tours overhead, McPhee stood in front of the group he assembled and shared a story about how one conversation with a Hall of Famer helped shape the franchise they built in the desert. McPhee admired how the Philadelphia Flyers went from an expansion team in 1967 to a Stanley Cup winner in back-to-back seasons in 1974 and 1975. In researching how to build

Vegas, he called Bobby Clarke, who played on the expansion team and also helped build the franchise as a general manager.

"There were different takeaways from the meeting, but one of the biggest was 'Make Vegas special,'" McPhee said onstage that night to his players. "Make it a special place to play in the NHL. Make it special for the players and their families. And that's what we've tried to do."

That special touch might take the form of something small, like being the only team to wear gray helmets or wear white gloves permanently. Or it's a larger thing, like an unyielding philosophy to do the right thing, no matter how difficult.

"There's a right way to do things and a wrong way to do things and there's no in between," McPhee said. "And we're going to do everything the right way."

Then he shared with his players an early meeting he had with Kelly McCrimmon. McCrimmon was originally hired in Vegas as an assistant general manager and it came during a time in which McCrimmon was emerging as a hot commodity for promotion from his spot as owner, coach, and general manager of the Western Hockey League's Brandon Wheat Kings. McPhee didn't know McCrimmon at all when it was suggested to him by scouts in the organization that he was worth a call. McPhee saw someone who didn't need a big checkbook to win in the WHL. McCrimmon was winning with scouting, managing, and coaching. McPhee dug some more. He called Mike Babcock, who he got to know through Hockey Canada, to get a scouting report because he heard Babcock and McCrimmon were good friends. At the time, Babcock was still the coach of the Toronto Maple Leafs under Lou Lamoriello.

What can you tell me about Kelly?

They chatted for thirty minutes and Babcock went through it all, a glowing assessment of what Kelly brought to the table as a manager and talent evaluator. McPhee thanked Babcock for the time and the thorough scouting report. Then Babcock tacked on one more piece of information.

By the way, we're trying to hire him in Toronto.

"I go, 'Fuck. Fuck. The next call this guy is going to make is right to Lou,'" McPhee said. "And he did."

There was also speculation that the Arizona Coyotes were interested in McCrimmon. And while each of those situations might have appealed to someone making the jump to the NHL, McPhee was quietly confident his offer was the best. For one, after five minutes of conversation, the two hit it off. They spoke the same language, had the same core beliefs. Plus, who else could offer to build an NHL franchise from scratch?

"I just sensed that Kelly, this was the right place for him to come to," McPhee said. "[The Maple Leafs] couldn't even define what they wanted him to do in Toronto with the group they had. I just said, 'Kelly, we're going to do everything together and it starts with expansion.'"

"I was fascinated by expansion," McCrimmon said. "My whole career has been drafting and developing and building teams."

The lure to build something from scratch was more than McCrimmon could resist. They both flew to scout at the Ivan Hlinka Memorial Tournament and met at the Vienna International Airport, which was the entry point for the tournament in Bratislava, Slovakia. It was at the airport where they shook hands for the first time to finalize the deal. Onstage at the ring ceremony, McPhee shared a conversation the two had early in their tenure working together. It was about the setup they both realized Vegas offered.

"Vegas is an easy place to live," McPhee said, his voice echoing slightly through the evening air. "It's easy to get around. We have amazing facilities. It's easy to get to them from your neighborhood, easy to get to your airport, and easy to get to your main rink downtown. You have wonderful weather here. Desert winters are amazing. It's attractive because there's no state income tax."

They realized they had every external ingredient to success. Supportive ownership. Loyal fan base. Incredible local logistics for players living in the area. Weather. Taxes. Name it.

"Kelly and I were talking about all those things and sort of said to each other, 'If we do our jobs here, if we do our jobs in getting the right players, and if we do our jobs in getting the right staff and everybody we want is low ego, intelligent, hardworking, and high-character people, great leadership—and we've done that all through our organization. It's been remarkable. . . . We've done every single thing we can, every day we've been here to win. And we won a Stanley Cup."

His final story onstage was about Foley. Deciding which names from the organization would be engraved on the Stanley Cup was a pain point. It always is. There are only fifty-two spots on the Stanley Cup for the winning team and there are hundreds of people who contribute to a franchise winning a championship.

"It was really hurtful for some people to not be on the Cup, and to tell people they're not going to be on the Cup, it breaks your heart," McPhee would say later. "There are people who deserve to be on there."

The players want to see their names on the Cup. They want to see their teammates. They want to see the people who help them survive the grind every day—coaches, the equipment managers, medical trainers. They don't want to see a bunch of names they don't know. So to avoid a battle that could linger all summer, McPhee worked with McCrimmon the first week after the Cup was awarded to submit a final list. About a week after the list was submitted, McPhee received a call from Foley. He had made promises to team investors about getting their name on the Stanley Cup if Vegas ever won a championship.

"I said, 'Bill, you're probably going to be mad at me right now, but I hope six months from now, you're thanking me, because some of those people don't belong on the Cup," McPhee said. "But the people who have their jobs on the line all year, all throughout the organization, they belong on the Cup. They earned it. And so that's what we've got to do."

McPhee said he'd take the fall from anyone angry. And then, when it came time to submit a list of who in the organization would receive a top-tier championship ring, McPhee pushed again. Typically, a professional team wins a championship and the players along with select support staff receive top-tier rings, often costing six figures each. An NBA team, for instance, might create thirty of those top-tier rings. The further you get away from the players, the lower the tier and the lower the cost of the rings handed out. McPhee submitted the request, and it was more than triple what an NBA team might give for tier one rings. His reasoning was simple: In three or six years, the amount of money spent in this moment won't matter to a billionaire. The night the rings are handed out, all people are going to think is that this is an owner who cares deeply about his staff.

"'They're going to think this is the greatest organization on the planet,'" McPhee said he told Foley. "'And they're going to talk about you as an owner that way. If you don't do it that way, some people are going to say you're cheap. Why, of all these times, would you get cheap on this? It may never happen again.'"

Foley's response?

"There was no hesitation," McPhee said.

On the night of the ring ceremony, McPhee shared some of those details.

"I think we're up to a hundred and four tier one rings," McPhee told the group. "We came up with the requests to make this happen for everybody and we didn't get any pushback. Had a few questions, but we didn't get pushback, but we made it happen. Everybody here tonight is getting a tier one ring."

After a couple more speeches, everyone got to see exactly what McPhee was talking about. Elvis impersonators started to pour out of nowhere, with millions of dollars' worth of jewelry in their hands. The actual Elvis was echoing loudly over the speakers surrounding the Wynn stage and pool singing "Viva Las Vegas" as the rings were being distributed. One by one, the names of players for the championship team were called, and all the Elvises—covered in rhinestones, collars up—made their way toward the players.

"Jack Eichel!"

"Jonathan Marchessault!"

"Mark Stone!"

"Alex Pietrangelo!"

The players opened the boxes and lifted them up. They slid the rings on, showed them off. They shed tears as they posed together for pictures. Huge smiles were everywhere. I walked over to McPhee to see if I could get a closer look at the ring.

"What a ceremony," he said, shaking his head, touched by the moment. He held out his hand. There were sixty-seven white diamonds on the helmet of the logo representing the total wins the Golden Knights earned en route to the Stanley Cup. There were another thirty-two diamonds representing each team in the NHL. There was a Stanley Cup made of diamonds surrounded by six stones representing each of the six seasons Vegas has played in its existence. The top detached to reveal a replica of the interior of the Golden Knights' arena. Inside the band is an inscription that reads "Cup in Six," a reference to Bill Foley's prediction before the team even played a single game. Nobody says what they cost, but there are replicas for sale for $75,000, which would cost someone a cool $7.7 million if they wanted to buy 103 of them to match the number of tier ones that Foley purchased for that night. Players were trying them on. They were sharing them with spouses and girlfriends. And while I suspected McPhee's ring would immediately go to a safe at the conclusion of the evening, I was wrong.

The next morning at the Golden Knights' practice facility, there was a local car wash and detailing company in the players' lot cleaning cars. Every week, these workers show up to detail the collection of Mercedes, Range Rovers, Teslas, and other luxury cars that fill the lot. When McPhee pulled up to park, he greeted the staff. He was wearing the championship ring from the night before exactly for a moment like this. He understood that there were people who were part of the team at every level, who deserved a firsthand look at the ring. He slipped it off his finger and encouraged the guys washing cars to pass it around.

"They were just flabbergasted," McPhee said.

We were sitting in his office at the practice facility and team headquarters in Summerlin, Nevada, just across the street from the Red Rock casino and near the Las Vegas Ballpark, home of the Triple-A Aviators. Nearly every player on the Vegas roster lives six to eight minutes away. We settled in for an extended conversation.

"How does it all feel?"

"To have this?" McPhee asked, holding up his hand with the ring.

I shrugged.

"Yeah," he answered softly, and gave a small laugh. "It's sort of conflicted."

McPhee speaks in a soft, low tone that speeds up when he's talking about something he's convicted about, and then trails off as he searches for just how much he wants to share. He's generally quiet and keeps a low profile. He's always been content to stay in the shadows, but is also cordial when you ask to chat. It can be hard to align the man across the desk with the player he was. Listed at five foot nine, 170 pounds on HockeyDB.com, McPhee won a Hobey Baker Award as an elite goalscorer in college hockey and then entered the NHL swinging.

"He turns pro and is fighting all these guys," McCrimmon said. "If you look at his fight card and you sit and talk to him, it's amazing."

Scott Stevens. Marty McSorley. A steady diet of Rick Tocchet. These weren't lightweights McPhee took on. Occasionally it carried over to his post-playing career. His former assistant GM Frank Provenzano, who worked for him in Vancouver and Washington, remembered one night during the 1999 exhibition season where he thought it would be safe to sneak away for a night of camping while McPhee's Capitals were on the road playing the Blackhawks. After a night in the wilderness, Provenzano turned his phone back on the next morning and the messages were piled up.

"The phone went cuckoo," Provenzano said.

There was a voicemail waiting for him from McPhee.

Uh, Francis, give me a call.

While playing what was supposed to be an ambassador exhibition game in Columbus, the Blackhawks loaded up their lineup with tough guys.

"They dressed a goon squad," Provenzano said.

The Capitals didn't. Because they brought a lighter, skilled team on the road to this game, one guy had to answer the bell for the Capitals in these fights. That guy was a six-foot-one winger from White River, Ontario, named Trevor Halverson, who had spent nearly a decade battling for time in the IHL, AHL, and ECHL before playing seventeen games with the Capitals the previous year. Halverson ended up getting a concussion that night and never played in the NHL again. Furious, McPhee stormed down to the Blackhawks dressing room after the game, looking for then–Chicago head coach Lorne Molleken. The result of the altercation was a black eye for Molleken, and McPhee ended up with a cut on his face and a missing arm on his suit jacket to go with quite the story in the local papers the next day. In classic Ron Wilson wit, the former Capitals coach told the *Washington Post* that the only thing that upset him about the incident was that McPhee didn't invite him to join the fight.

"I think he would have seen the whole staff march down there," Wilson said. "I'm 100 percent behind what George did. George went in there and stood up for our team."

The NHL fined McPhee $20,000 and suspended him for a month. So, behind the low profile and the soft-spoken answers exists a deep well of passion and emotion. It's emotion that surfaced as he answered what the ring and the Stanley Cup meant to him.

He started by sharing the reaction that met his expectations. He expected the initial euphoria that came with the celebration with players and his staff. He expected the civic pride that swelled in Vegas when two hundred thousand people lined Las Vegas Boulevard as they celebrated the championship with the fans while riding in double-decker buses and convertibles down the Strip. He even expected the personal validation he felt when he was rewarded for sticking to his convictions and seeing the fruition of really hard decisions he had to make along the way.

"What I didn't expect was the impact that the—and I don't want to get soft in my old age—the love that the Stanley Cup generates," McPhee said. "What it does for your family and friends. I'll never look at the Stanley Cup the same again."

He had taken the Stanley Cup to his hometown of Guelph, Ontario, where he got to share it with his extended family and friends. He was able to reconnect with the kids he used to play road hockey with when he was ten years old. There were family members he hadn't seen in years.

"It's a lovefest when everybody gets together. A lot of people haven't seen each other, you know? It's the crowd that would show up at a funeral, but they're pulling the Stanley Cup out of a case and not your body," McPhee said, and then let out a laugh. "I never understood that, and you have to go through it, I think, to really experience it. I remember driving away from Guelph, going to Toronto the next day, and had this weird feeling in my chest.

What's going on? Geez, at my age, I sort of feel homesick today. I miss all these friends. I miss the family. But for the Stanley Cup, I don't know if any of that happens where they all come together. That's been the most meaningful."

When McPhee's Golden Knights were playing his former team in the 2018 Stanley Cup Final, a small group of Capitals players sat around a table on the day of Game 5 and talked about the opportunity ahead of them. They didn't know for sure that their lives were about to change forever that night. They didn't know they'd be at a club at 4 a.m. celebrating a championship that would bond them until the end of time. They did realize that a day like that doesn't always come around. Chandler Stephenson, Brooks Orpik, and Jakub Vrana started going through a list of Hall of Fame players who had never won a Stanley Cup. As the conversation continued, it really hit home just how rare a day it was for them. For McPhee, the pain of losing the series to the Capitals was familiar. Twice, he'd guided a team he built to a Stanley Cup Final and twice he lost.

"I just think when you come close and lose and maybe if it's further down the road in your career, you have a much greater appreciation for winning," Orpik said, while telling the story of that 2018 Capitals team.

That was clearly the case for McPhee. Sitting in his office, a championship ring on his finger, the pain of the past could fade away and reemerge as wisdom for what it takes to get there. The pain converted into lessons on how to build a great organization. At one point, McPhee nodded his head toward the Golden Knights logo on the wall in front of him and reflected on the powerful brand he, Foley, and the group in Vegas had built in a short period of time. The night before, he had sent a note to

Foley that said simply: *You've built one of the finest organizations in all of sports.*

It doesn't happen without the wisdom that the failure in Washington provided. For someone like McPhee, whose thirst to keep learning is constant, there's a natural growth that takes place over time. He's a guy who brings books with him during his vacations to Martha's Vineyard. He also believes strongly in the power of observation. He's around a lot. He has breakfast every morning with McCrimmon and they do it in a way that's visible to players and staff so that there are daily touch points with nearly everyone in the organization. He's always felt that's just part of being a manager. The presence, to him, is a prerequisite.

"You have to do it. It's an all-the-time job. It just is," McPhee explained. "You have your day shift, you have your night shift. You work holidays. You work weekends. The summers are busier than the season."

You're there to observe. And you're there to deal with the inevitable issue of the day.

"There's always something that has to be addressed. Always," he said. "But even the little things, they have to be addressed. It's how you keep people on the right path."

When it comes to players, McPhee has learned that they want to be in a good organization. He's also learned that players want accountability. They want structure. They want to be a part of something special. During one of the first gatherings of players following the expansion draft, McPhee shared a PowerPoint presentation with the group that showed exactly how things were going to go with the Golden Knights. There were very clear guidelines on what management would expect. On what coaches would expect. Players were expected to wear a jacket and tie for every game. Wear a suit when you get on the team plane and when you get off the plane. McPhee believes that when a player starts putting on a suit at three thirty on the afternoon of a game, something happens with their mental preparation. It symbolizes going to work. And he let the team know, if there was an issue, he was going to address it. He believes in accountability. He also believes that when you lose accountability, entitlement seeps in. He saw it happen for a moment of time in Vegas.

If you listen closely, you start to pick up on how McPhee makes those corrections, how he interacts with his players in a way that addresses problems without putting them on the defensive. The first Golden Knights season, McPhee heard about one particular player in the dressing room bothering teammates with his jokes. The player thought he was being funny, but he wasn't. The humor was actually hurtful. McPhee called him in for a chat.

"You're a young guy," he told him. "I would have appreciated it when I was your age if an older guy like me was sitting down and trying to explain something to me. I want you to listen to me. You're rubbing people the wrong way. You're not being nice. You're trying to have fun, you're trying to be part of this and do the right things, but you're not. You're not. People dislike what you're doing and you've got to stop."

McPhee gave a few specific examples of jokes that landed the wrong way and asked if it all made sense to the player. The player's response? He thanked him. He said nobody had ever done that for him.

"It's no different from years ago in New Jersey with Lou [Lamoriello]. Brendan Shanahan was late for a couple of things and everything else. He brought him in and told him to get a Day-Timer and told him to get organized and worked with him,"

McPhee said. "Young guys, they don't know how to be pros. There aren't many who know how to be pros. They need to be taught."

Some lessons come with a tough conversation in a manager's office, others come with experience. When McPhee was running the Capitals, he went through a series of coaches during the Alex Ovechkin era that never quite got the team where it needed to be in the playoffs.

Bruce Boudreau might have been the best hire, promoted from the AHL to replace the fired Glen Hanlon. But when Boudreau was fired, the organization believed he'd taken the team as far as he could. Then came the Dale Hunter hire, a marriage that didn't go beyond the single season in which Hunter replaced Boudreau. Hunter instilled defensive structure. He got the team to sacrifice in the name of winning. But he left, preferring to work for his team in London, where he was calling the shots and close to his family. It was the next hire that forged a conviction with McPhee about the coaching hiring process that is as strong as any he has in management.

"I am not going to fuck around on coaches," McPhee said. "We're getting the best coach available. And that's all there is to it."

That means zero hesitation to make changes when necessary.

"If you see something that you just don't think is going to work, then you're not doing your job. You can't look the other way and hope everything is going to be okay," he said. "It doesn't work that way. The hard decisions were made and there's no other way to do it."

The Golden Knights have been unapologetic on this front. Gerard Gallant was the first coach of the Golden Knights. He took them to a Stanley Cup Final. He won the Jack Adams Award in 2017–18. He was gone by 2020. Peter DeBoer, considered one of the NHL's best tacticians, was hired to replace Gallant. He went 98–50–12 with Vegas. He was gone by 2022. Bruce Cassidy was hired to replace DeBoer. McPhee knew Cassidy would bring accountability. He also knew he wasn't always easy to play for, but that's how he wins. It was Cassidy who raised the Stanley Cup in 2022, which should buy him some time. In theory.

If you want to trace McPhee's no-nonsense stance on coaching, go to the day Adam Oates was introduced as the Washington Capitals' head coach on June 27, 2012. In a navy pin-striped suit with a red tie, McPhee shook hands with Adam Oates in front of more than seventy media members, who crammed in to see the former Capitals star return to the organization and try and lead them beyond the early playoff disappointment that was starting to define the group.

As McPhee listened to Oates talk and take questions from the assembled media, he had a sinking feeling this wasn't the right hire. During the interview process, McPhee talked to Craig Berube and was impressed. Berube ended up leading the Blues to the Stanley Cup in 2019. Dean Evason, then a Capitals assistant, gave a strong interview, too. But, in McPhee's mind, the coach should have been a relatively unknown former lawyer winning a bunch of games in the AHL. McPhee interviewed Jon Cooper and loved him.

"Wanted to hire him," McPhee said.

McPhee, Brian MacLellan, and Cooper sat together in the Capitals' hotel suite in Pittsburgh during the week of the 2012 draft. The interview lasted a couple hours and then McPhee invited Cooper to stay for dinner. Dinner extended into a hangout with the three watching a baseball game in the suite that went long enough that Cooper was trying to figure out a polite exit strategy. But the longer the meeting went, the more Cooper became convinced he was getting the Capitals job. That's why Cooper was surprised when it took more than a few days to hear back from McPhee.

"Then George calls. I didn't get the job," said Cooper, who got the impression this wasn't entirely McPhee's decision. "He was being professional by not saying certain things."

Cooper would win back-to-back Stanley Cups in 2020 and 2021 with the Tampa Bay Lightning. His success justified McPhee's belief that he was the right choice. And made McPhee completely convinced that he wouldn't go against his instincts with a coaching hire again. Oates wasn't a great fit and often didn't seem to mesh with the players McPhee acquired, most notably Martin Erat. There were public debates over player usage, lineup changes, and Oates's decision to move Alex Ovechkin to right wing.

Ultimately, both Oates and McPhee were fired in late April 2014.

It was a costly lesson. But it only cemented the belief that there was a certain standard to which Vegas had to operate and it was the only way to do business. And when it came to building the roster, there was a window of time in which that high standard came into play in a way the league had never seen.

It was the summer of 2017 and then–Islanders general manager Garth Snow was having conversations with the Edmonton Oilers. Snow was interested in acquiring Jordan Eberle, a four-time twenty-goal scorer for the Oilers. There was a deal to be had if he was willing to move Ryan Strome, which he was.

There was a holdup.

"I can't do anything until after the expansion draft," Snow said during trade conversations.

Why?

"I gave my word to George and we can talk after."

The George was George McPhee. And the after was after the expansion draft.

After hiring Kelly McCrimmon the previous August, McPhee sat down with his new assistant GM and split the league in half. McPhee got fifteen NHL teams. McCrimmon got the other fifteen. Each guy was charged with getting to know those franchises inside and out.

"I've referred to it as taking your undergrad and MBA in one year," McCrimmon said. "As fascinating as I expected expansion to be, you could multiply it by fifty."

They dug in. They studied the personnel of each of the teams they had under their purview. They studied their analytics, their salary cap situation. They started meeting with and talking with the general manager on each of their teams. Years later, McPhee would share these details in an interview with Brian Burke at his annual sports business conference and on a podcast with Bob McCown and John Shannon that are both a great listen. The Golden Knights leadership would meet often with the entire staff in the front office's war room. The pro scouts were in the room. The younger hockey operations staff. The analytics team. Everybody had a say.

A software developer for the Golden Knights put together a program where anyone from the front office could change an input, like the number of defensemen a franchise might protect, and it would update the entire Vegas matrix. About once a month, they'd do a mock expansion draft. Sometimes they started alphabetically. Sometimes they'd start at the bottom with the Winnipegs and Washingtons. Every time, they learned something. Every time, it got a little bit easier.

But as the pro scouts got more viewings of the players on their list and McPhee and McCrimmon increased the number of conversations with the general managers on their list, it became clear who would be available.

After clarity came fear.

If the season ended and all the NHL general managers made trades to solve their expansion draft protection issues, there would be a massive redistribution of talent across the entire NHL landscape. It would thwart all the plans the Golden Knights were putting into place to build the future of their franchise.

So they got to work preventing it.

Between cap issues or talent protection issues or both, McPhee and McCrimmon identified ten teams that they believed would have to make a move either with them or with another NHL team before the expansion draft. They set out to make sure it was their franchise getting the benefit of that squeeze and nobody else. They were able to make deals with nine of them in the weeks leading up to the expansion draft.

During the first trade, McCrimmon mentioned to the opposing general manager that the deal that had just been agreed to was conditional. If that team made another trade, the deal was off. They also needed to keep it quiet. That became the model.

"We started doing secret deals with teams," McPhee told Burke. "It wasn't disclosed to anybody."

"That's cagey by him to read all the tea leaves and know that all the trades could affect him," Snow said.

In the end, the Islanders sent Mikhail Grabovski's contract, a 2017 first-round pick (fifteenth overall) and a 2019 second-rounder to the Golden Knights in order for them to take goalie Jean-François Bérubé. The Islanders felt like any of those players they might lose in the expansion draft was worth a first-rounder. The Golden Knights used that 2017 first-rounder to select Erik Brannstrom, a young defenseman who was the centerpiece in a trade that brought captain Mark Stone to the organization. Along with an eventual Stanley Cup.

In all, those nine trades allowed them to add William Karlsson, Alex Tuch, Marc-André Fleury, and Shea Theodore. It loaded the Golden Knights up with draft picks. It also showed just how much McPhee's word was trusted around the league. These trades had to be kept quiet. It took an immense amount of trust in McPhee's word to follow through on each of them.

"Your word is everything. If you can't stand by your word, you're not going to last long in the business," Snow said. "And I would put him right up there with Lou [Lamoriello]. You don't need a contract with Lou. You just need a handshake."

McPhee had nine of those handshakes. Handshake deals that changed the course of the franchise. It really was a master class in preparation and execution.

"Yeah. It was incredible. It was incredible," McPhee said. "The way we operated it. It was pretty special. And sort of a glimpse of what was to come."

This was the birth of the Misfits, the group that surprisingly advanced to the Stanley Cup Final in its inaugural season. As impressive as building it was, the move that involved more resolve was the dismantling of that team. The coach was eventually fired. Popular goalie Marc-André Fleury was traded. Many key pieces were moved in the name of demanding the best, and this approach wasn't roundly applauded. People in the game questioned the cost of culture, of disrupting a close team, of trading beloved players. These weren't popular moves.

"I've always believed as a manager that you need to objectively assess your team. It's easy to overrate your team as a manager and it's easy to underrate your team as a manager. But you have to manage what your team is," McCrimmon said. "Year one changed expectations here. Our assessment was that we sort of caught lightning in a bottle."

McCrimmon countered criticism by saying they weren't pursuing every shiny object following that first year. They believed the moment they acquired Mark Stone that it made them legitimate Cup contenders. They believed strongly that Cup winners need a top-pair defenseman and number one center, so they acquired Alex Pietrangelo and Jack Eichel.

It was only about filling the requirements of a championship-caliber team, raising the talent level to what they believed it needed to be. It's about expectations and not shying away from the difficult decisions required to reach them. McPhee wanted this franchise to be different, he wanted it to be special. That was the motivation behind every hard choice, it's what pushed him through the toughest of them.

"You see something you don't think is going to work, you have to make the change," McPhee said. "That's where people started beating us up. Trading popular players, people started beating us up. But . . ."

He stopped a moment.

Then raised his hand with the championship ring.

ACKNOWLEDGMENTS

There were times I was convinced this book would never get written. There were travel restrictions coming out of a global pandemic. There was the sale of the company I worked for to the *New York Times* and the emotional investment that came with a transition to new ownership. There was a new job within that company that came with heightened demands on time and mental energy. And disturbing stories that emerged from the world of hockey that made me think hard about highlighting team management at all.

But right now, I'm so glad I did. I learned so much. About building, managing, friendship, perseverance, faith, the pursuit of greatness, kindness, and sacrifice. I'm appreciative for the opportunity to share it with others. Thank you to everyone who participated in these interviews. To everyone who shared their time, their insight, their trust in connecting me with loved ones, and for their willingness to share what they've learned with those interested in the sport. Or even those just interested in what it takes to lead.

There's so much work behind the scenes that goes into these connections, so a sincere thank you to Sergey Kocharov, Anu Rangappa, Nate Ewell, Brant Feldman, Mike Sundheim, Kimber Auerbach, Pete Albietz, Jeffrey Sanders, Kevin Wilson, Steve Keogh, and Scott McNaughton for everything.

Also, this doesn't get done without the gentle persistence of my agent, Brian Wood. Thanks for the check-ins, encouragement, and occasional push. The same goes for the team at Simon & Schuster Canada: Nicole Winstanley, for your support seeing this through; Jim Gifford, Rob Sternitzky, and Rachael DeShano for all the hard work on the editing side. Kevin Hanson and Justin Stoller, your faith and encouragement at the outset of this project is what got it off the ground.

Thank you to my bosses, Steven Ginsberg and Seb Tomich, at *The Athletic* for only once pointing out the irony of me skipping a team event at night to work on a book about team building. And to the two founders of *The Athletic*, Adam Hansmann and Alex Mather, for providing me the opportunity of a lifetime to help build and manage a team we'll remember for the rest of our careers.

Special shout-out to the staff of the Clinton-Macomb Public Library for providing a quiet place to write and sparing me the dirty looks I deserved for leaving the building as you locked up behind me at closing time.

And lastly, my family.

To my parents, you instilled a love for learning, reading, and leadership that set this all in motion. You taught me how to work, how to have fun, and mostly how to love. Thanks Dad and Mom.

Calvin, I know you understood when I wasn't around late at night or on weekends because you're off working even harder on your own dream. It's so fun to watch it all come to life. Cameron, I know you understood, too, because you might be the only person on earth who enjoys the quiet corner of a library to sit, read, and write more than I do. I know something great will grow from that passion. Cormac, sorry for the games of football I had to cut short to get this done. I'll meet you out front.

Finally, Cassie. Writing this meant more nights alone, having me disappear for stretches during vacations, and incoming calls at the worst possible times that had to be taken. And yet, you were there at the finish line, pushing me across. I can't even begin to tell you what your support means to me. I love you.

INDEX